Transform Your Life Instantly

36 Steps to Reach Greater Heights

Jayaprakash Nagathihalli

Transformation Mentor

AUTHOR'S NOTE

Special Features of the Personality Transformation Book

This work is presented based on the author's research and experiences. Most of these words and ideas are already familiar to everyone. The aspects have been categorised and explained based on the author's real-life experiences. These concepts have been tested practically in several trainings and workshops. Videos have also been provided via YouTube, and a positive impact has been evident everywhere. This book is offered to you with the good intention that such positive transformations will happen for you too, making your life more fulfilling.

Personality

Everyone is an individual. Those who possess good qualities and values have a strong personality. Personality is what fragrance is to a flower. A person's behaviour and speech help us identify their personality.

Transformation

As mentioned in the *Bhagavad Gita*, Change is the law of the universe. When we talk about change, there are two options: becoming better from worse or becoming worse from better.

However, transformation signifies only *positive change.* Therefore, mere change is not enough; transformation is what truly matters.

Reaching New Heights

The following quotes inspire us to aim higher:

1. Our destination is not among the stars, it lies within us. - *Shakespeare*
2. Progress is not enough; achieving excellence should be man's goal. - *K.S. Nisar Ahmed*
3. The chair you sit in is not great; you must become great. – *Shri Siddeshwar Swamiji*
4. You will never see a rainbow if you keep looking down. - *Charlie Chaplin*
5. Don't sit, don't stop, don't descend; keep climbing. - *Masti Venkatesha Iyengar*
6. See the Highest, Aim the Highest & Reach the Highest. - *Swami Vivekananda*

Praveen Rabakavi

A thinker, actor, and director who has provided complementary and attractive illustrations for all chapters of this book. His dedication is truly inspiring, and his illustrations have given this book a distinct appeal. Thank you.

MacBook Air

By personally typing this entire book, revising, and rearranging the content using a new laptop, I was able to shape this work thoughtfully. This journey of playing with words has been enjoyable. My heartfelt thanks to my laptop, and to Mrs. Impu for assisting with technical support.

Dear Reader

You have consistently responded positively to all our books. Many of you have shared how adopting our ideas has helped you reach greater heights in life. Such feedback inspires us to write more. Some of you have also participated in our classes and workshops, buying extra copies to give to others. Salute to you all! Reading will uplift your life. Best wishes to you.

Books Published so far in Kannada Language

1. *Nudigannadi*
2. *Solugalige Anjadiri*
3. *Keelarime Enu? Yeke? Hegge?*
4. *Anukshana Anubhavisi*
5. *Udyoga Kaushalyagalu*
6. *Tiruvugala Arivu*
7. *Ananyate Ariyiri*
8. *Sadhakara Chandana*
9. *Sahitya Chandana*
10. *Vyaktitva Chandana*
11. *Nirupane Nirupisi*
12. *Jeevanotsaha*
13. *Vyaktitwa Darpana*
14. *Vyaktitwa Parivartane*
15. *Lifu Namdene*

Books published in English Language

1. *Fear Not Failures*
2. *Inferiority Complex*
3. *Celebrate Every Moment*

With great joy, we present this book to readers who have warmly received our previous works. Many of you have shared valuable feedback via letters, emails, and phone calls, which has further inspired us.

Author's Experience

30 years of recognition in the field of *personality development*. Over 10 lakh people have been trained, and in the past 5 years, we have also reached many people through online classes. Our ideas continue to spread through social media. Seeing some of our trainees emerge as achievers has further fuelled our enthusiasm.

Read this book completely and share your feedback. For **Online or Offline training** or guidance, feel free to contact us.

Contact Information:

Bengaluru
Jayaprakash Nagathihalli

Date: 15th January 2025

Mobile: +91 9886081188

Your suggestions and feedback are always welcome:
Office Mobile Numbers: +91 9341259267 / +91 9620303000
Email: smilingjp@gmail.com

Find us on social media: *Jayaprakash Nagathihalli*

YouTube Channels:

1. *Jayaprakash Nagathihalli*
2. *Transformation Unlimited*

———————————————————————————

CONTENTS

1.

FROM INDISCIPLINE TO DISCIPLINE

Discipline is the foundation of personality

Discipline is the first and the foremost aspect of personality development. This is because the more you progress toward inculcating discipline, the more changes you can observe in your overall personality.

Discipline encompasses many aspects

It includes life purpose, goal setting, time management, planning, and many other elements that are interconnected and complementary to each other.

Discipline and Time

The connection between time and discipline is evident and undeniable. As you respect time, time will respect you in return.

A schedule is like a fence that protects your time

A well-planned day can make your entire life beautiful. Therefore, creating a schedule to make each day organized will support you immensely.

No plan can have quality without discipline

For any activity to be of high quality, discipline is a must.

With discipline, you win; without it, you fail

When we analyze failures, the most common reasons we find are indiscipline and laziness.

People with indiscipline have never achieved greatness

Laziness, inertia, and reckless behaviour will never lead us to success.

Self-discipline is essential

We must first focus on and prioritize personal discipline.

Those who aim for great heights must overcome their weaknesses

Many achievers have faced numerous challenges and difficult circumstances in their lives, overcoming them to grow and become legends. Likewise, history teaches us that talent combined with indiscipline can lead to failure. Hence, it is important to ensure you don't falter when striving for the summit.

In cricket, there is a saying: *No matter how great a player becomes, he must bend down to pick up the ball running toward the boundary.* This implies that in both sports and life, following rules and maintaining discipline is essential to standing tall.

"Faith is not superstition"

- Swami Vivekananda

—————————————————-

2.

FROM QUESTIONS TO ANSWERS

"A person's personality is shaped

Not by the answers he gives,

But by the questions he asks."

- Voltaire, French writer

No question, no answer

Every answer in life arises only when you ask questions of yourself or others.

A child cries, and only then does the mother feed it

This analogy is widely accepted. Similarly, questions inspire others to engage in communication.

Do not accept without questioning - Dr. H. Narasimhaiah

Dr. H. Narasimhaiah had a large question mark painted in his room with the motto "Do not accept without questioning." Throughout his life, he asked essential questions for society and exposed many misconceptions and false beliefs.

Self-awareness begins with questions. Who am I?

Ramakrishna Paramahamsa and Ramana Maharshi often advised their disciples to ask themselves, *"Who am I?"* By frequently questioning yourself, you encounter diverse answers that shape your personality.

Asking What should I become? Reveals many answers

Questions about life's purpose, goals, roles, and aspirations bring deeper meaning to our existence. When you reflect on what you should become, life either reveals its purpose or you define it for yourself.

Seek experts for solutions to life's problems

Everyone encounters challenges, but for every problem, there are experts who can help. For instance:

- Doctors for medical issues,
- Lawyers for legal matters,
- Psychologists for mental health,

- Personal counsellors for individual concerns,
- Life coaches for life skills.

Don't hesitate to speak openly with them or spend money for their guidance.

Curiosity drives questions

Children ask more questions because they are naturally curious. Keep this curiosity alive in your life.

Answers always begin with a question

This is a fascinating truth. If you seek answers, you must first ask questions.

Lawyers in court ask questions to uncover answers

During trials, lawyers continuously ask questions to extract the truth. This highlights the importance of questions in seeking clarity.

Answers through interviews

Be it job interviews, radio or television interviews, the basis is always rooted in questions.

The 5 W's & 1 H formula

The majority of our lives revolve around these six fundamental questions:

- Why?
- When?
- What?
- Who?
- Where?
- How?

The Q-Factor: Are we asking the right questions?
Reflect on whether your questions are appropriate and relevant. Instead of asking, *"Why me?"* start asking, *"What's in it for me?"* Focus on how to make the best use of any given situation rather than dwelling on why it happened to you.

> *"Learn from YESTERDAY,*
> *live for TODAY,*
> *I hope for TOMORROW.*
> *The important thing is not to stop QUESTIONING."*
>
> **- Albert Einstein**

———————————

3.

FROM COMFORT ZONE TO EFFORT ZONE

"When I was on the throne,

I was inexperienced,

But when I stepped down,

I became a reservoir of experiences."

- Prema Bhat

The Big Fence of Comfort

Understand the difference between temporary peace and real satisfaction.

Dangers of Staying in the Comfort Zone:

1. No growth at all.
2. Missed opportunities.
3. A stagnant personality.
4. Feelings of inferiority take over.

5. Over dependence on others instead of self-reliance.
6. Success remains out of reach.

Were we born just to stay comfortable?
Most people aim for comfort, but ask yourself should you seek comfort when you have the potential for greatness? If you put in the effort, success follows. If obstacles arise, let them come. If you fail, so be it. Keep moving forward.

Don't Become Like Stagnant Water

Take the **Dead Sea** as an example since its water doesn't flow, nothing can survive in it.
Remember the saying: **"Flowing water is fit to drink."**

Effort Eliminates Fear

Fear fuels negativity. Worrying too much about obstacles and failures weakens you. **The journey of success itself is victory.**

Why Hesitate to Take Responsibility?

Many people refuse promotions because they don't want to step out of their comfort zones and take on more responsibility.

Pain & Pleasure Principle

To experience greater happiness, you must endure small pains.

Intrinsic vs. Extrinsic Motivation

Think about the Indian gooseberry: **It starts sour but turns sweet.**

Key Takeaways:

7. Everyone starts as a dependent.
8. Humans alone strive to improve.
9. Don't be like the person who hangs themselves from the tree their father planted.
10. Research and invention happen only through effort.

The Final Message:

Step out of your comfort zone.
Your comfort zone benefits no one not even you.
If you refuse to step out, you will be left with regret.
The comfort zone is the death zone.

Life begins at the edge of your comfort zone.
Great things never come from comfort zones.
Success is waiting for you just outside of it.

"Short-term pain for long-term gain."
"He who wants to catch fish must not mind getting wet."

"Sit and watch, even mountains will melt.
Take small steps, and mountains will be under your feet."

- Hariprasad

————————

4.

FROM USELESSNESS TO USEFULNESS

"Why lie dormant?

Why burden the earth?

Laziness is enough!

Rise up and work deeply to live like a king!"

- V.C. Irsang

No wisdom yet?

The first wisdom hasn't even dawned,

And by the time it does,

Your life is over

Don't let this happen, right?

No one is useless; they are simply used less

This saying holds so much truth, doesn't it? Human bodies, the "hardware," are almost the same for everyone. But it's the "software" that differs. Decide for yourself what kind of "software" you need in your life; it can transform your entire journey.

Gratitude: The Debt of Thanks

Many have contributed to shaping our lives: parents, teachers, relatives, friends, and well-wishers. By seeking their guidance and accepting their corrections, we can find direction in life. Similarly, many achievers have become guiding lights for others. Seek such mentors, follow their advice, and apply it to your life. Never forget their contributions, and express your gratitude.

95% of Humans are Underperforming

It is estimated that 95% of people use less than their potential, while only 5% fully utilize their abilities. The author has written books and conducted training and mentoring programs with the goal of inspiring readers to join that 5%.

Separate Yourself from the Crowd

To stand out from the crowd and move toward leadership, you need continuous effort and perseverance. Unlike sheep that follow blindly, recognize this distinction and tap into your immense inner potential. Others can only walk beside you but cannot walk your path for you. *It's your road and yours alone. Others may walk it with you, but no one can walk it for you.*

Small, Consistent Efforts vs. Doing Nothing

Doing something, no matter how small, is better than doing nothing at all. Small efforts eventually lead to bigger accomplishments.

Don't Live Someone Else's Life

This is your life. Live it for yourself.

Better Late than Never

Be the author of your life and the reader of your mind.

The more you understand yourself, the less you will seek approval from others.

Stay Alert

Life is like riding a bicycle. To maintain balance, you must keep moving.

Social Responsibility

Your personal achievements aren't enough unless they benefit society. True success lies in uplifting others because we are interdependent.

The Power of One

- One **tree** can start a forest.
- One **song** can spark excitement.
- One **smile** can rejuvenate an atmosphere.
- One **star** can guide a ship through the darkness of the sea.
- One **person** with the right attitude can achieve wonders.
- One **pure soul** can uplift the whole world.
- One **person's character** can inspire humanity.

Have enthusiasm but avoid agitation.

Don't make excuses; keep trying.

Eliminate what is unnecessary.

Remember:

"Do something, Mankuthimma"

– D.V.G.

"It's better to wear out from work

than rust from idleness."

- Swami Vivekananda

"Ships are safe in the harbor,

but that's not what ships are built for."

"Who has ever walked by sitting still?"

– Raghavanka

Understand that self-effort is superior to fate.
You are more valuable than you think.

The two most important days in your life are:

the day you are born and

the day you find out why.

- Mark Twain

————————————

5.

FROM POWERLESS TO POWERFULNESS

The Unique Nature of Energy

Everyone possesses a special energy, which must be identified. The human body is a bundle of energy reservoirs. Understanding and harnessing these energies can empower you:

- **Law of Vibration**
- **Law of Attraction**
- **Power of Movement**

SWOT Formula

Analyze your:

- **Strengths**
- **Weaknesses**
- **Opportunities**
- **Threats**

This self-awareness makes life more meaningful and balanced

KASH Formula

To grow, focus on:

- **Knowledge**
- **Attitude**
- **Skills**
- **Habits**
  Regularly refine these aspects to become your best self

Heart and Mind Coordination

When the thoughts of the mind align with the emotions of the heart, communication improves, and negativity is reduced.

Smile Concept

A smiling face radiates positivity. Cultivate the habit of smiling naturally, spreading joy and optimism wherever you go.

Life Lessons from Hardships

Hardships, failures, and pain should be viewed as experiences that refine you, just like a rough stone polished by life's challenges.

Power Dressing

Your attire reflects your personality. Dressing well and appropriately, known as "Power Dressing," enhances confidence and leaves a strong impression.

Unveiling Personality

Laziness is your enemy. Continuously work on personality development by attending training programs and reading books. Learn from experts around you and seek their guidance for self-improvement.

The Power of Communication

- Your **words**, **writing**, and **body language** hold immense power.
- Using appropriate language at the right moment can be very impactful.
- Writing can help resolve challenges and clarify thoughts.
- Confident body language conveys strength, dignity, and seriousness.

Six Dimensions of Personality Development

1. **Physical**
2. **Mental**
3. **Intellectual**
4. **Emotional**

5. **Spiritual**
6. **Financial**

Value of Time

Time is the most precious asset. Respecting time brings respect from the world. Time management instills discipline and ensures you achieve your goals effectively.

Recognize Your Strengths

"Don't say there's no power within you.

It's in your eyes, where it gleams.

It's in your blood, where it flows.

It's in your sweat, where it shines.

It's in your words, where it impresses.

It's in your writing, where it emerges.

It's in your name, where it grows mighty.

Don't showcase your strength. Prove it when the time comes!"

- Katte Erriswami

Empower Yourself

Discover your uniqueness and personal strengths. Realize that all power lies within you. You can achieve anything, overcome self-doubt and rise above limitations.

You Are the Powerhouse

You are a vast reservoir of all kinds of energy. Recognize, awaken, and utilize it to its fullest potential.

You Are the Creator

You are responsible for your life. You write your destiny. You are the sculptor of your future. Channel your energy towards your goals and aspirations.

"Climbing to the top demands strength,

whether it is to the top of Mount Everest or

to the top of your career."

- A.P.J. Abdul Kalam

————————

6.

FROM DREAMS TO GOALS

"Our destination is not in the stars, it is within us."

- William Shakespeare

Where There's a Will, There's a Way

We've grown up hearing, "Where there's a will, there's a way." Undoubtedly true! If we move our dreams toward achievable goals rather than just dreaming, we take the first step toward success.

Live with Dreams, Not Fear

Fear often holds us back from moving forward. Overcome your fears, push them aside and conquer them. Both mental and physical activities can help in this process. Learning skills like public speaking can significantly boost confidence.

The Rainbow of Dreams

A rainbow is mesmerizing but fleeting. Similarly, dreams that captivate our minds in a state of awareness need to be recognized and utilized for progress.

Keep the End in Mind

Where are our efforts heading? What ultimate result are we aiming for? These questions should constantly guide our actions.

Focus on Quality, Not Quantity

"Instead of digging ten wells, dig one well deeply to find water,"

says a wise proverb. Similarly, focus on quality rather than spreading yourself thin across multiple goals.

How Many Goals Should You Have?

- **5 Goals:** As suggested by Warren Buffett.
- **3 Goals:** Plan A, B, and C.
- **2 Goals:** Plan A and Plan B.
- **1 Goal:** Focus on one goal that contributes to your growth.

Power of Focus

Concentrate all your activities on your main goal. Even if you engage in diverse activities, your attention must always return to the primary objective.

A New Mindset Brings New Results

A shift in mindset changes outcomes. There's no doubt that new ways of thinking lead to fresh achievements.

The Target Attracts the Arrow

The sharper your goals, the more magnetic they become, drawing resources and focus towards them. Pay undivided attention to your goals.

Vision Board to Action Board

Create a Vision Board that represents your goals. Place it where you can see it daily. This subconsciously influences your mind and drives action.

Learn from Yesterday, Live Today, Hope for Tomorrow

Self-belief plays a crucial role in our lives. At times, we limit ourselves by thinking we're incapable. But this isn't necessary sometimes, even if we don't achieve the entire goal, we make significant progress. Activities you love often grow into major successes in your life.

"Within the seeds of your desire is everything necessary for it to blossom to fulfilment. Let a person radically alter his thoughts, and he will be astonished at the rapid transformation it will effect in the material conditions of his life. Each and every step one takes must move him/her toward the cherished goal."

A Dream Worth Chasing

"A dream that makes you lose sleep is worth pursuing."

-A.P.J. Abdul Kalam

Activity:

What do you want written on your tombstone? Write those words and live your life accordingly.

———————————-

7.

FROM PREPARATION TO SUCCESS

The Importance of Preparation

Before embarking on any journey, we meticulously plan, don't we? Similarly, preparation is crucial for navigating life effectively. Success thrives on well-laid plans and diligent efforts.

"Learn from yesterday, live for today, and hope for tomorrow."

Preparation Leads to Success

Preparation involves three key stages:

1. **Planning (Preparation):** Outlining the path ahead.
2. **Rehearsal:** Simulating situations to gain confidence.
3. **Practice:** Perfecting skills through repetition.

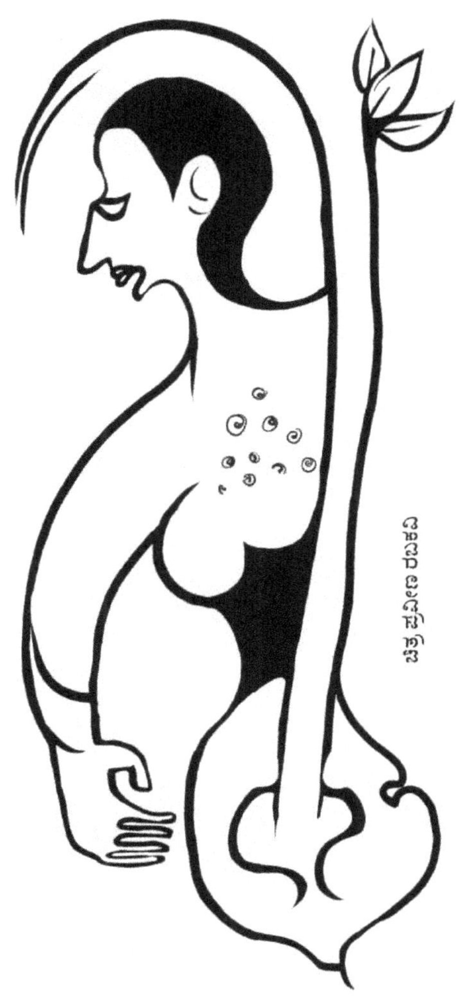
ලේකම බණ්ඩාර පිදු

These steps are essential for:

- **Examinations**
- **School and College Milestones**
- **Competitive Exams**
- **Various Stages of Life**

Bruce Lee's Wisdom

"I'm not afraid of the man who has practiced 10,000 kicks once,

but I'm afraid of the man who has practiced

one kick 10,000 times."

--Bruce Lee

This emphasizes the power of focused, repetitive practice in achieving mastery.

The Story of the Bucket and Kung Fu Training

This beloved tale illustrates the importance of perseverance and preparation:
A father leaves his son with a Kung Fu master to learn martial arts. The master instructs the boy to repeatedly strike water in a wooden bucket every day for a year. Frustrated by the monotony, the boy plans to return home. However, when his friends question his progress, he angrily strikes a table with his

hands, splitting it into two. Only then does he realize the master's teaching his hands had become as strong as stone through diligent practice.

Skills Pay Bills

Your skills are your currency. The more skills you acquire and refine, the more opportunities and rewards you can access.

Hope for the Best, Prepare for the Worst

While aiming for positive outcomes, always be prepared to face challenges. Resilience and readiness are key to overcoming unexpected obstacles.

What Goes Around Comes Around

Just as seeds sown yield corresponding fruits, our efforts determine our results. Consistent, honest efforts will eventually bring success.

Sweat or Bleed

"Sweat in preparation, or bleed in the battle."

This powerful military adage underscores the significance of hard work and preparation. Putting in effort during preparation minimizes risks and ensures success.

Key Takeaways

- Preparation is the foundation of achievement.
- Repetition and focus lead to mastery.
- Skills are lifelong assets invested in them.
- Balanced optimism and preparedness build resilience.
- The effort you invest today shapes your outcomes tomorrow.

Success is not a sudden event; it's the result of diligent preparation. Stay ready, stay focused, and embrace every challenge as an opportunity to grow.

—————————-

8.

FROM WORRIES TO CONSTRUCTIVE THOUGHTS

Worry Weakens, Thought Strengthens

"Worry doesn't reduce tomorrow's problems;

it steals today's strength."

- **Anonymous**

Our mind is a powerful tool. It can be:

- **A garden of blooming ideas.**
- **A compass guiding life.**
- **A source of invincible strength.**
- **A machine creating meaning.**

Nourish your mind with positive thoughts, just as the body needs food. Transform it into a **factory of creativity** rather than a **storehouse of worries**.

ಚಿತ್ರಕೃಪೆ: ಪ್ರವೀಣ ರಬಕವಿ

From Worry to Growth

Worry leads to stagnation, but thoughtful reflection propels progress.

When a million things bring you down, find one reason to rise.

Convert pressure into pleasure and steer your energy into meaningful pursuits. Remember:

- Worrying is akin to worshipping problems it attracts negativity.
- Focus on **small joys** that act as the roots nourishing the tree of life.
- Practice **simple living and high thinking.**

Choose Between Worry and Thought

"Worry burns like fire; thoughts bloom like flowers.

The choice is yours."

--Hariprasad

Harnessing the Power of the Mind

With focused thinking, you can achieve remarkable outcomes:

- Resolve problems with clarity.
- Sharpen your concentration and memory.
- Cultivate creativity and positive attitudes.
- Expand your thinking to greater horizons.

- Relieve mental stress and find enthusiasm for life.
- Overcome fears and insecurities.
- Experience joy and satisfaction.

Writing as a Path to Clarity

Writing down your thoughts bridges your mind and hand, leading to transformative actions. By documenting:

- Problems and their descriptions, you externalize your worries.
- Life events, you gain perspective and see patterns.
- Emotions, you foster personal awareness and growth.

This process improves not just your responses but also your ability to navigate challenges effectively.

The Mind Shapes Reality

What you plant in your mind grows into your life. Every challenge presents an opportunity. Shape your mindset, and you shape your future.

"Progress thrives on thought,

while its absence fosters barriers."

--Dr. Abdul Kalam

Key Takeaways

- Worry and thought are two sides of the same coin.
- Thoughtful reflection leads to progress, creativity, and resilience.
- Transform your mental habits by focusing on positivity and writing.
- Leverage the power of your thoughts to move from worry to wisdom, from stagnation to success.

"Sweat saves blood, blood saves lives, but brains save both."

- Edwin Rommel

—————————

9.

FROM SPECTATOR TO PLAYER

Life Is Your Game, Play It

"Don't just watch others play; play in a way that the world celebrates you."

-Coach Ramakant Achrekar to Sachin Tendulkar

Life isn't about watching others live. It's about actively participating, leading, and creating moments worth cherishing.

Life as a Game

- Life is a **game**, a stage, a **laboratory of experiments.**
- It is an intersection of various events and opportunities.
- Your perspective defines how you play your role in this grand game.

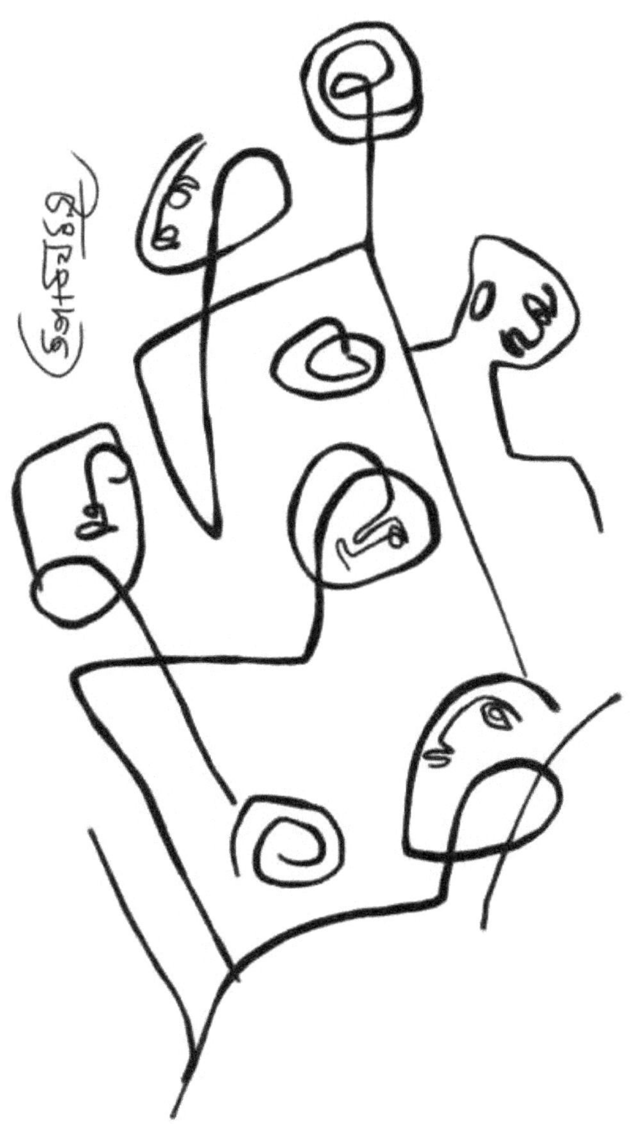

Success Belongs to Players

> *"Only* players' experience victories or defeats.
>
> Spectators can merely clap or complain."

To achieve success:

- Step into the arena of action.
- Participate actively rather than passively observing life pass by.

Activity Keeps Sickness Away

Those who are constantly engaged in purposeful work rarely experience despair or idleness.

Be dynamic:

- Keep transitioning from one meaningful activity to another.
- Prevent boredom and lethargy from creeping into your life.

Live in the Present Moment

> *"Yesterday was a canceled cheque, tomorrow is a promissory note, but today is ready cash."*

To excel as a player:

- Immerse yourself completely in the present.
- Avoid distractions of the past or uncertainties of the future.

Be Your Own Hero

Be a real hero in your life, not a reel one.

You are the protagonist of your life:

- Recognize your worth and lead by example.
- Seek validation from within before expecting it from others.

Master Your Field

Whatever your field of interest:

- Strive to become a skilled and knowledgeable player.
- Continuously improve and master your craft.

Time to Stop Watching and Start Playing

"Enough of watching, listening, and waiting. It's time to play, speak, and act!"

*- **Katte Erriswamy***

Life rewards those who take initiative. Step forward and actively shape your destiny.

Takeaways

- Life is not a spectator sport; you must actively participate to win.
- Engage fully in the present to make the most of your efforts.
- Be the hero of your journey and master your domain.

Call to Action

It's time to shift from being a passive observer to an active player. Make your presence known, take bold actions, and let the world witness the champion within you!

———————————————-

10.

FROM VAGUENESS TO CLARITY

"Only those who pay attention

to the little details

become great people."

- Jayaprakash Nagathihalli

Focus on the Small Things

Greatness begins by paying attention to the small things, the finer details that shape the whole picture.

Clarity through Knowledge

- As **knowledge** increases, **clarity** increases.
- With knowledge comes the understanding of purpose and direction.

Using Knowledge to Correct Errors

- **Glasses (SPECTACLES):** Just like glasses correct vision errors, knowledge helps to correct the flaws within ourselves.
- We should use the power of knowledge to remove the mental and personal flaws that cloud our understanding.

Priority and Awareness

- Understanding the importance of **priority** helps enhance our awareness and focus.
- When we have clear priorities, our vision becomes sharper, and we align our actions toward our true purpose.

Direction and Guidance

- **Direction** is essential: Awareness of the path we are on is crucial.
- The **mountain** in the distance is not clear unless we approach it. Similarly, clarity comes when we move closer to our goals.
- Just like **car headlights** guide us on the road, we must keep a **dynamic movement** toward clarity in our lives.

The Three Mirrors of Guidance

- **Three Mirrors**: The left, right, and rearview mirrors of a car provide guidance about the path ahead.
- In life, we too must focus on the present, anticipate the future, and learn from the past. Keep your attention on all three.

Perception of Beauty

When asked which country is the most beautiful, TV N. Murthy, who has travelled to over 120 countries, answered: ***Every country is beautiful, you must see each one as it is.***

- Beauty exists everywhere, and it's all about how we choose to perceive things. Life is about perspective, and clarity is shaped by how we see the world around us.

Overcoming Obstacles

- Just like **melted snow** on a road allows us to move forward, we must clear obstacles in our lives and continue progressing.
- Life's difficulties may slow us down, but they should never stop us from moving forward.

Be True to Yourself

Others may mislead us, but we should never mislead ourselves.

- **Self-honesty** and clarity come from within. Don't let outside influences distort your path. Trust your inner direction.

Saying 'No' Clearly

Learn to say NO when you want to say NO.

- **Clarity in communication** is key. Saying no when necessary is important for personal growth. Don't hesitate or over-explain; stand firm in your choices.

Takeaways

- **Focus on the details** to grow and build your path to success.
- **Increase clarity** through knowledge, awareness of priorities, and active guidance from the past, present, and future.
- Don't allow external distractions to cloud your vision. Stay true to your purpose and values.
- Learn to communicate with **clarity and conviction**, especially when setting boundaries.

Final Thought

To move from vagueness to clarity, you must actively shape your vision, correct internal flaws, and take responsibility for the direction you choose in life. Clarity is not something that comes passively; it's built through conscious decisions and focus.

———————————-

11.

FROM LACK OF KNOWLEDGE TO GREAT KNOWLEDGE

The Importance of Enlightenment

Eliminating ignorance and embracing the path of wisdom is the foundation for personal and societal growth. As Dr. B.R. Ambedkar said, education is the most powerful weapon to uplift the standard of living.

Awareness

Awareness is the guiding light in our lives. As poet B.M.

Srikantaiah expressed in his verse:

> *"O Compassionate Light, come forth,*
>
> *hold my hand, and guide me"*

This calls us to move from darkness to light.

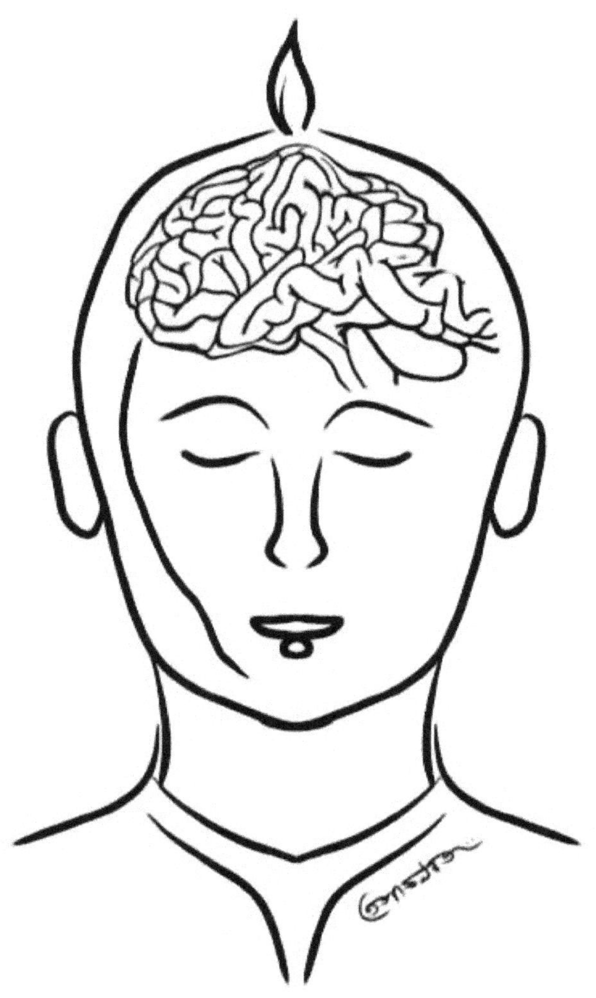

The Importance of Education

Education shapes individuals into disciplined and cultured beings, contributing significantly to societal progress and national development. The saying, ***"Money is great; knowledge is greater"*** reminds us that education is more valuable than wealth.

The Need for Lifelong Learning

Learning is a continuous process. Be it through exploration, reading books, or mastering new technologies, those who persistently pursue knowledge without complacency will reach the pinnacle of success.

The Role of Books

Books are invaluable resources for gaining knowledge. The habit of reading not only broadens your perspective but also paves the way to success.

Technology and Training

Leveraging technology to enhance life requires constant recalibration:

- **RE-ALIGN**: Realign goals.
- **RE-INVENT**: Reinvent strategies.
- **RE-DESIGN**: Redesign approaches.
- **RE-POSITIONING**: Reposition for growth.

- **RE-AFFIRM**: Reaffirm commitments.

Focus on Needs, Avoid Distractions

By avoiding unnecessary activities and concentrating solely on our goals and needs, we can achieve excellence in life.

Knowledge and Life

As Mahendra Kurudi eloquently states:

"Knowledge resides within us, ignorance resides within us, God resides within us, the devil resides within us"

Only by embracing awareness can we truly attain a meaningful human life.

The journey from ignorance to wisdom is the ultimate weapon to reach the pinnacle of greatness.

———————————-

12.

FROM PAIN TO PLEASURE

"We can't learn without pain."

- Aristotle

Pain and pleasure are like two sides of the same coin, as reflected in the message of our Ugadi festival: **"Neem and jaggery" (symbolizing bitterness and sweetness).** The English song lyric, **"Enjoy the rain, enjoy the pain,"** carries a similar sentiment. Whether it's the body or the mind, pain is universal.

As Charlie Chaplin once said:

"I cry only when I act in the rain."

Joyful Pains

Certain pains bring ultimate happiness:

- Childbirth
- Tireless efforts for the welfare of society

ಚಿತ್ರಕೃಪೆ: ಪ್ರವೀಣ ರಬಕವಿ

- Creative activities
- Therapeutic practices like acupressure, acupuncture, deep tissue massage, and foot massage
- Physical exercises, which might cause initial discomfort but lead to long-term benefits

"Every pain gives a lesson,

and every lesson changes a person."

- Dr. A.P.J. Abdul Kalam

Pain Builds Strength

Just as fire tests gold, hardships test the courage of individuals. Challenges mould ordinary people into extraordinary achievers.

- **Happiness Through Pain**: Pain teaches resilience and forges strength.

"The pain you feel today will be the

strength you feel tomorrow."

The Essence of Happiness

Happiness stems from various facets of life:

- **Emotional**: Smiles, laughter, and joy

- **Relationships**: Love, friendship, and companionship
- **Social**: Connections and organizational activities
- **Physical**: Health and fitness
- **Intellectual**: Continuous learning and growth
- **Spiritual**: Meditation and positivity
- **Economic**: Active and passive income sources

Gratitude is the key to happiness.

Happiness lies in perspective. Simple values like **simplicity, patience, and peace** are the three mantras of joy.

From Bitterness to Sweetness

Life's journey, from bitterness to sweetness, mirrors the process of milk turning into butter.

"If you feel pain, you are alive. If you feel others' pain, you are a human being."

Victory Through Pain

"No pain, no gain."

- Insults might inspire determination, and experiences teach life lessons. As poet **Da. Ra. Bendre** said:

"If life is Boiled, one may become Bendre (great)."

Arunima Sinha remarked:

"Severe hardships can prepare an ordinary person for extraordinary goals."

The Natural Path from Pain to Joy

The human body has an innate ability to transform pain into pleasure. Our body naturally produces elements to reduce pain. Emotionally, crying helps release grief, paving the way for healing and joy.

From Crying to Laughing

"Happiness is like a vine that grows within the heart,

not outside."

- Khalil Gibran

A child enters the world crying, while a person leaves the world amidst tears.

"A smile transforms negativity into positivity."

Balancing Life

Life is a balancing act, with ups and downs for everyone. Happiness lies in appreciating the simple things in life and embracing humour through plays, movies, and videos.

As poet **G.S. Shivarudrappa** writes:

"Nature never tires of its fresh creations."

And M. Srinivasa Murthy aptly said:

"There may be wrinkles on the face, but there shouldn't be wrinkles in the field."

Life is about finding harmony

in every moment, transitioning

from pain to ultimate joy.

————————

13.

FROM PROBLEMS TO SOLUTIONS

"Why worry about the obstacles

ahead on an unseen path?

Face them with courage."

- Kayyara Kiyyannarai

Key Guidelines

1. Be part of the solution, not part of the problem.
2. Don't blow things out of proportion.
3. Focus on solutions, not problems.
4. Move from confusion to conclusion.

Personal Reflection

What problems have I solved for myself?

- Health problems
- Energy issues
- Career challenges

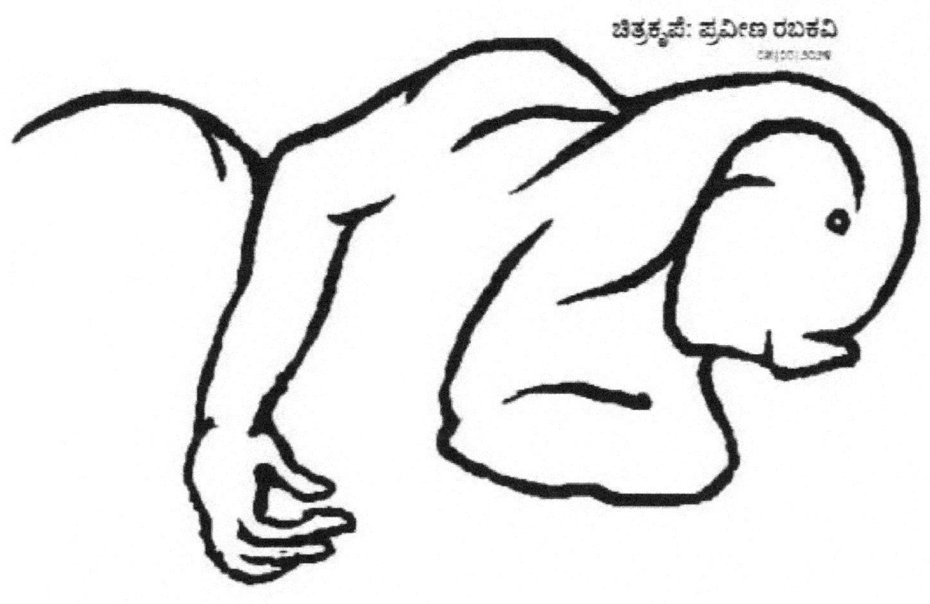

ಚಿತ್ರಕೃಪೆ: ಪ್ರವೀಣ ರಬಕವಿ

- Leadership hurdles
- Communication gaps
- Relationship struggles

What problems do I care about deeply and want others to avoid?

- Financial difficulties
- Time management issues
- Aspiration conflicts
- Instant decision-making challenges

Every Problem Has a Solution

Do not aim for a perfect solution's accept small improvements. Instead of thinking, there's only one way, adapt to better alternatives.

Mindset for Problem-Solving

1. Identify the problem.
2. Focus on resolution.
3. Solve the issue.
4. Learn from the experience.

Benefits of Problem-Solving

- Increased self-confidence
- Freedom from thoughts of despair
- Joyful and peaceful future
- Mental tranquility
- Awareness of personal priorities
- A fresh perspective on life

Understanding the Mind

1. Conscious mind

2. Subconscious mind

3. Superconscious mind

"If we dwell on problems, we become the problem. If we move toward solutions, we become the solution."

- Hariprasad

Steps to Overcome Problems

1. Stay active and involved.
2. Don't worry about trivial issues.
3. Analyze whether a situation is truly likely to occur.
4. Accept unavoidable circumstances and move forward.
5. Let go of the past and don't stir up settled matters.

6. Think and act as if you're already happy.
7. Don't waste time worrying about unchangeable people.
8. Turn misfortune into opportunity, like making lemonade from lemons.
9. Perform a good deed daily to bring a smile to someone's face.
10. Work as hard as you can, but also enjoy what you do.
11. Solve problems rather than avoiding them.
12. Stop complaining and start acting. Take small, steady steps.
13. Understand that most problems stem from either overthinking or lack of action.

Thinking Patterns

1. Short-Term Thinking vs. Long-Term Thinking

Balance immediate goals with long-term visions.

2. Uniform Thinking vs. Informative Thinking

Incorporate diverse and informed perspectives.

3. Fast Thinking vs. Slow Thinking

Learn when to make quick decisions and when to deliberate.

Key Metrics to Focus On

- **IQ**: Intelligence Quotient
- **SQ**: Social Quotient
- **EQ**: Emotional Quotient
- **AQ**: Adaptability Quotient

Problems Are an Inseparable Part of Life

Solving them is an art.

"If something is important to you,

you will figure out a solution."

Let life's struggles shape your strength and resilience.

As Emerson aptly said:

"The more challenges you face, the sharper your mind works."

———————

14.

FROM DANGEROUS TO ADVENTUROUS

"Do not fear shadows,

for they simply indicate that

somewhere nearby a light shines."

- Ruth E. Renkel

Adventure Strengthens Us

Engaging in activities like:

- Car racing, bike racing
- Trekking and mountaineering
- Parasailing and bungee jumping
- Wildlife photography
- Sports and recreational pursuits

These activities invigorate life, fostering a spirit of courage and resilience.

Embrace Acceptance Over Expectations

Excessive expectations often lead to dissatisfaction. Cultivate acceptance and appreciate life as it is. This shift in mindset can transform your perspective on living.

Opportunities Depend on Readiness

Opportunity relies on circumstances, but choice depends on mindset.
Be prepared when preparation meets opportunity, success becomes inevitable.

Dare to Take Risks

"Ships are safe in harbour,

but that's not what ships are built for."

Only those who take risks can achieve greatness. If the path is difficult, it signifies your goals are bigger than imagined.

As the poet *Raghavanka* said:

"Who dares to walk forward, not just those who sit still, will reach their destination."

Overcoming Fear

An adventurous spirit helps dispel inner fears. Fear loses its grip when faced with calculated risks and a courageous attitude.

The Spirit of Perseverance

- Keep moving forward. Never start with **"This is impossible."** Begin with **"I can do this."**

- Soldiers demonstrate this mindset willing to sacrifice for the nation while showing extraordinary bravery in adversity.

Stay Alert and Prepared

- Learn from the **Border Security Force (BSF)**: Always remain alert and ready for action.
- This level of preparedness helps make clear, confident decisions in life.

Calculated Risks

Take risks, but calculate and evaluate them first. For instance:

- Cars rest on the ground if they fail, but airplanes in the air demand greater preparation and precision.

- Build the courage to face measured risks.

Lessons in Risk-Taking

When challenges intensify, resilience grows:

"When the going gets tough, the tough get going."

Taking risks builds immunity against fear and strengthens your ability to navigate life's uncertainties.

Shift Your Focus

Instead of worrying about how you will die, focus on how you are living.

Adventure is not the absence of fear but the decision to act despite it. Let courage guide you from danger to discovery, from fear to fulfilment.

————————

15.

FROM FAILURES TO SUCCESS

"Failure is not a true defeat;

it is an experience."

- Jayaprakash Nagathihalli

The Reality of Failure

In life, everyone encounters failures in various forms and at different stages. However, for those who look ahead and seek the path forward, failure becomes merely an experience. Changing how we perceive failure is essential. Embrace failure as a stepping stone to growth.

The Role of Self-Confidence

Self-confidence plays a pivotal role in overcoming failures. Building confidence involves mental and physical practices, such as:

- **Public Speaking Skills:** Learning to articulate ideas can enhance self-assurance.

- **Life Skills Training:** Workshops and courses both online and offline can expand perspectives, helping you identify areas for improvement and personal growth.

Cultivating Enthusiasm for Life

Sustaining enthusiasm is vital for resilience. If individuals above 90 years of age can live with energy and purpose, so can you! Explore *"Jeevanotsaha" [ENTHUSIASM]* by the same author for insights into the power of vitality.

Be Active and Receptive to Learning

- **Participate in Development Programs:** Join personality development workshops.
- **Be a Man of Action:** Take proactive steps in your personal and professional life.
- **Seek Guidance:** Don't hesitate to approach well-wishers or experts for advice. External perspectives can offer clarity and solutions to challenges.

Powerful Sayings

"The only thing that makes a dream impossible is

the fear of failure."

- Italian Proverb

"A comforting word during failure is more valuable than an hour-long congratulatory speech after success."

- Dr. M. Govinda Pai

"Life changes after a significant setback."

- Aparna Vastare

Life is for Living, Not for Giving Up

Life is a precious gift. Understanding its value and purpose enables a more fulfilling existence. This perspective enhances joy, emphasizes the importance of time, and diminishes thoughts of ending life under any circumstances. The Hindi movie *Chhichhore* beautifully illustrates this idea.

Key Takeaways

1. Failure is a temporary setback, not a permanent defeat.
2. Confidence and enthusiasm are powerful tools for recovery.
3. Seeking guidance and participating in self-development programs accelerate success.

4.   Never fear failure, fear stagnation.

For more inspiration, read *"FEAR NOT FAILURES"* Book by Jayaprakash Nagathihalli.

————————

16.

FROM INFERIORITY TO SELF CONFIDENCE

"The knowledge in your head and the confidence in your heart are more important than the lines on your palm or the marks on your body."

- Swami Vivekananda

Overcoming Inferiority

"Rise above, my friend. Let go of hesitation, for within your mind lies boundless strength."

-Jarganahalli Shivashankar

Inferiority, in various forms, haunts many people. To overcome this, we must first identify the roots of these thoughts and then confront them. Some may worry about their appearance, while

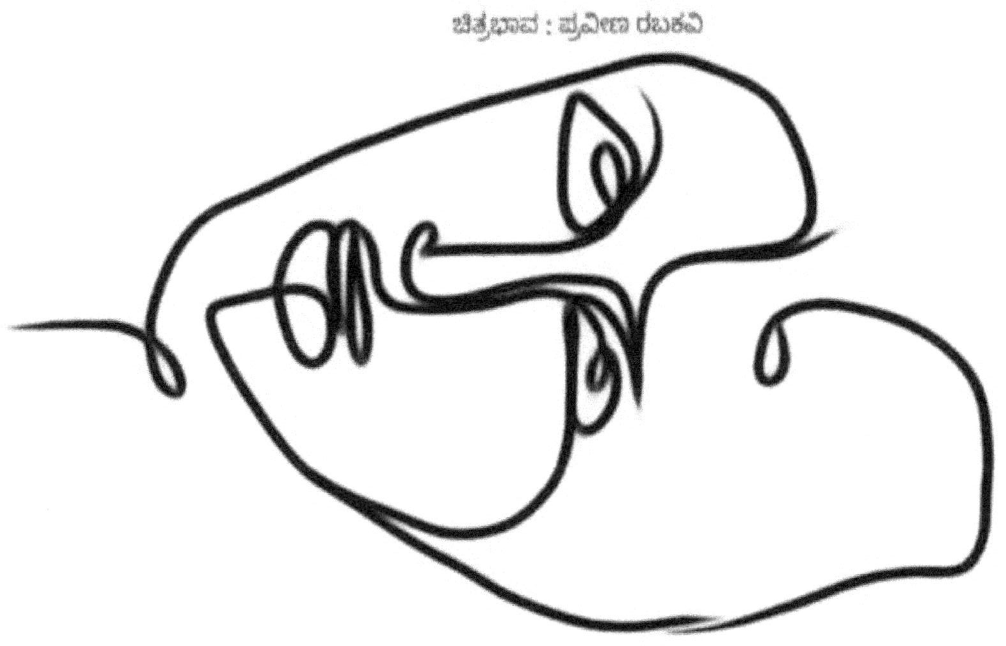

ಚಿತ್ರಭಾವ : ಪ್ರವೀಣ ರಬಕವಿ

others may fear aging, lack of education, or proficiency in English. Financial concerns, lack of respect from family, or poor health can also plague many. Life in a rural area or in comparison to others may also trigger feelings of inadequacy. For many, complaining becomes a daily routine.

But the truth is, opportunities for growth are abundant, and we must seize them actively. There's no reason to stay in the shadows of inferiority when we have the potential for improvement.

The Power of the Mind

Self-confidence, mental strength, and a broad mindset are deeply connected to how we manage and control our thoughts. Belief in oneself is essential for fostering this change. Consistency in activities and focusing attention on our goals will guide us toward building the strength needed to overcome inferiority.

The Essence of Confidence

Confidence is not about external factors; it's about an internal belief.

"When you fall, it's inferior.

When you rise, it's self-confidence.

Like a scale that balances' this is confidence."

- Hariprasad

Tips to Overcome Inferiority

1. **Prioritize Small Things:** Pay attention to the little details that build your personality.

2. **Adopt a Positive Mindset:** Cultivate optimism, as it shapes your behavior and reactions.

3. **Celebrate Uniqueness:** Appreciate what makes you different; it adds value to your personality.

4. **Be Authentic:** Embrace your true self, rather than trying to be someone you're not.

5. **Learn the Difference Between Right and Wrong:** This clarity will enhance self-assurance.

6. **Develop Good Habits:** Strong habits form the foundation of confidence.

7. **Trust Yourself:** Self-belief is the cornerstone of overcoming doubts.

8. **Accept Change:** Understand that change is a natural part of growth.

9. **Seek Wise Advice:** Be open to receiving guidance from trusted sources.

10. **Practice Gratitude:** A positive outlook attracts positive outcomes.

11. **Seize Opportunities:** Don't hesitate to take the leap when opportunities arise.

12. **Be Persistent:** Consistent effort is key to achieving success.

13. **Don't Hesitate:** Move forward without fear of failure.

The Train of Success

Success is like a train: it requires hard work, focus, and dedication. Luck might be a passenger, but the engine that drives it forward is self-confidence.

Life should be...

"Sweet like words,

Light like flowers,

Noble like the cow."

-DVG

For more insights, explore *"INFERIORITY COMPLEX" Book* by Jayaprakash Nagathihalli.

—————-

17.

FROM SPEECH TO ACTION

"The meaning of our words

comes from our actions."

- K.P. Poornachandra Tejaswi

Action Speaks Louder Than Words

In the world, many people talk endlessly. We often encounter those who speak much more than is necessary, and sometimes, unnecessarily. While words are important for communication, their true meaning is revealed through our actions. When compared, action outweighs speech. You must agree with this without action, words are meaningless. Those who speak and act are given more respect. If we fail to realize this, we risk becoming mere talkers. Hence, the relationship between speech and action is critical.

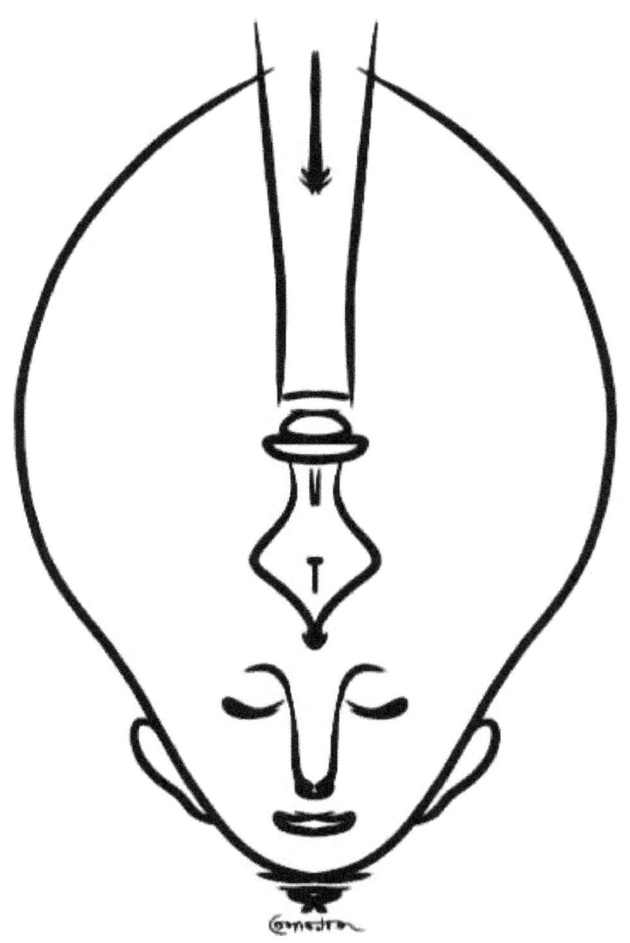

Action is the Key for Transformation

This is a concept that everyone must understand. Every point in this text relates to the power of action. Without action, everything becomes meaningless.

Work Brings Happiness

There is an undeniable relationship between activity and happiness. As Basavanna famously says, "Kayakave Kailasa" (WORK IS WORSHIP). In engaging in meaningful work, you will find more joy in life.

"Mantras Do Not Ripen Mangoes"

This proverb conveys a sharp, insightful message. No matter how many mantras you chant, mangoes will not ripen unless you take the necessary steps. Similarly, transformation only happens if we actively work toward it.

Be Practical, Be Action-Oriented

Don't just read from a book. Life is about being practical. The truth is not merely something to be understood; it must be experienced through action. Life is like the sea. Some catch pearls, others catch fish, and some merely dip their feet. The point is, whatever you strive for, you will achieve. Focus on what truly matters.

Words are Like Coins, Actions are Like Notes

In today's world, actions that are performed silently are more essential than words that are spoken. Words are like coins: they make noise. But even though notes are of higher value, they don't make any noise. Focus on enhancing your value, and let your actions speak for you.

An Empty Vessel Makes the Most Noise

Like an empty vessel that makes the most sound, people who are full of words but lack substance can be easily identified. What matters is what you want to symbolize with your life.

Actions Over Words

"Speech is just sound;

silence is purity.

The one who does and acts is the true one,

and the one who does neither is the lowest."

The Power of Good Company and Good Deeds

Good company and good deeds are essential. Education should not only cultivate intellect but also stir the heart. We need intelligent, kind-hearted people, not just knowledgeable ones.

When wisdom and kindness come together, everything becomes powerful and beautiful.

The Example of Manji - A Man of Action

"Tab Tak Todengi Nahi, Tab Tak Chodengi Nahi"

- Manji, the Man of Action.

Manji, in an effort to reduce the strain of bringing water from a distant place for his wife, carved a path through a mountain, thus making the way easier. This true story has been depicted in the Hindi movie *The Manjhi.*

The Power of Work Over Words

"Hands that work are superior to hands that merely greet."

-Biche

"No matter the profession, whether king or peasant, all labor is sacred."

-Kuvempu

"When debating, it is not the volume of voice that matters,

but the essence of the matter."

-Rumi

The Harmony of Thoughts, Words, and Actions

"Happiness is when what you think, what you say,

and what you do are in harmony."

-Mahatma Gandhi

Attempt May Be a Failure, But There Should Not Be a Failure of an Attempt.

This powerful sentiment reminds us that even when actions don't lead to success, the effort itself holds great value. It is through trying and acting that we learn, grow, and move forward.

————————-

18.

FROM POOR TO RICH

"Being born poor is not a mistake,

but dying poor is."

- Bill Gates

Sources of Income

- **Work**
- **Profession**
- **Hobby-turned-career**: Writing, Copywriting, Content Marketing, Social Media, YouTube
- **Skills**: Language, Speech, Presentation
- **Entrepreneurship**
- **Heart Wealth**

Negative Thoughts About Wealth

There are common misconceptions about wealth:

- "I can never make money fast."

- "Rich people are bad."
- "Rich people earn money through wrong means."
- "Wealth is a bad thing."
- "Rich people are cheaters."

Why Should You Aim to Be Wealthy?

- A better life for your loved ones
- Travel opportunities
- Ability to help others
- Become your own boss
- Freedom of time

Poverty is not Destiny

"Poverty is not about pace, it is not about limits, and it is not about fate. Try to change it, and see how life changes!"
Hariprasad

Earn, Save, Grow

- To earn, you must explore various ways to do so.
- Save as much as possible.
- Know where to invest to grow your capital.

Quantifying What You Need

Understanding how much money you need is crucial. Once you have clarity, you can begin earning towards that goal.

The Value of a Folded Note

Even when money is folded, its value doesn't decrease. I once saw a Rs.100 note, and I joked that it's just a piece of paper, but the note replied, "You're right, but I have never seen a trash bin!"

This illustrates that money holds value regardless of its form.

Skills Pay Bills

The more skills you develop, the more money you can earn. Your skills will determine your financial success.

If People Believe, They Will Buy

- Build relationships
- Create trust
- Develop desirability
- Establish credibility
- Build a favourable environment for yourself

Financial Levels (Stages of Financial Growth)

1. **First Level**:
   - Individuals earn a salary but spend more than they earn.
   - Result: Constant debt, living in financial struggle.

2. **Second Level**:
   - Individuals can clear debts but are left with no savings.
   - Result: Just getting by, no improvement or savings.

3. **Third Level**:
   - Individuals earn enough, pay off debts, and save a small amount.
   - Result: Unable to invest the savings wisely, leading to stagnation.

4. **Fourth Level**:
   - Individuals earn enough, pay bills, and save significantly.
   - Result: Wise investments, financial stability, and long-term growth.

Rules for a Wealthy Mindset

- **Money is a tool**: Understand how to use it wisely.
- **Respect money earners**: Learn from those who have achieved financial growth.

- **Prioritize spending**: Spend only on things that are truly important.
- **Continuous learning**: Always improve your financial knowledge.
- **Consistent evaluation**: Regularly review your spending, savings, and investment strategies.
- **Avoid comparisons**: Don't measure your financial progress by others' wealth.

Avoid Scarcity, Think Abundance

- The mindset of scarcity limits growth, while abundance opens doors to greater opportunities.

How to Increase Your Income (10 Ways)

- Brands reaching out to you
- Events and workshops
- Programs or courses
- Public speaking engagements
- Merchandise marketing (selling your own products)
- Affiliate marketing (specific opportunities)
- Coaching
- Social media posting
- Advertisements

The Harder Your Money Works for You, the Less You'll Have to Work for Money.

"It's Better to Work Harder Than to Take Loans"

- Jayaprakash Nagathihalli

By adopting a mindset of financial growth, improving skills, and making wise decisions, one can shift from a state of poverty to wealth. The goal is not just to accumulate wealth, but to use it wisely for the well-being of oneself and others.

————————

19.

FROM SMALL THOUGHTS TO BIG THOUGHTS

"Those who think small, remain small;

those who think big, become big."

- Jayaprakash Nagathihalli

Low Aim is a Crime

"Low aim is a crime," as stated by Jawaharlal Nehru.

Never consider your capabilities as limited. Everyone has the potential to achieve greatness. The key is to recognize and believe in your abilities. Always work towards your goals with a clear focus and trust in your beliefs.

Set Big Goals and Focus on Them

When you set big goals, your mind will start aligning itself towards them. In today's world, it's easier than ever to reach any corner of the world through the internet. You can make your mark on the global stage with the right focus and determination.

Constantly Stimulate Your Mind

Success doesn't depend on the size of your brain; it depends on the size of your thoughts. Your thoughts influence the size of your bank account, happiness account, and general satisfaction in life. A leader is someone who makes decisions with clarity, acting as a human machine capable of impactful decisions.

Think Big and Achieve Big

The idea that "you reap what you sow" holds true. If you plant big thoughts, you will naturally see big results. Big ideas lead to big accomplishments, a simple yet powerful truth.

Simple Living, High Thinking

Living simply and thinking deeply elevates your character. This mindset helps you understand life's truths and often inspires others to live humbly while striving for higher knowledge. Many have found their calling and achieved greatness through this principle.

"The Mind is not a vessel to be filled, but a fire to be kindled."

-Plutarch

A Secret of Life

- Roads have speed limits.
- Banks have money limits.
- Exams have time limits.
- But thinking has no limits!

So, **think big** and achieve big. There's no ceiling to the power of thought.

Respond to Insults by Growing and Living Well

Instead of engaging in quarrels with those who insult you, the best response is to grow and live a successful life.

Your success is the best reply.

Make Mental Ability to Make History, Not Just Record It

Don't just be a part of history, be the one who shapes it with your thoughts, decisions, and actions. Create a legacy that goes beyond mere documentation. Think big and leave your mark on the world.

This section emphasizes the importance of aiming high, thinking big, and continuously developing one's mindset. Small thoughts limit your potential, but by embracing a mindset of greatness, you unlock unlimited possibilities. Success and greatness are

born from thinking beyond boundaries and always striving for
more.

102

———————

20.

FROM NEGATIVITY TO POSITIVITY

Change Your Perspective, Change Your Reality

"When your perspective changes,

your view of the world changes."

The way we perceive things is incredibly impactful. Once we shift our perspective, the reality we see around us also changes. Understanding this is crucial for personal growth.

Your Attitude Determines Your Altitude

Attitude is the key to success.

While knowledge, skills, and good habits are essential, without a positive attitude, reaching the heights of success becomes difficult. Your mindset determines how high you can go in life.

The Arts as Supporters of Positivity

Cultural activities like literature, music, dance, and drama play a vital role in building a positive environment. These creative pursuits help foster a positive atmosphere and encourage constructive thinking.

Support Positive Aspects of Life

We should align ourselves with positive elements in life. By doing so, we naturally move toward a positive mindset. Let positivity drive your thoughts and actions.

Share Good Thoughts, Keep Negative Ones Personal

Share positive ideas openly, but keep critical feedback or negative thoughts to yourself. Address areas that need improvement in private, as this will help you win others over in a more constructive way.

Gratitude Kills Negativity

Incorporating a mindset of gratitude into your life helps keep negativity at bay. Gratitude naturally fosters a positive environment, encouraging growth and improvement.

Be Aware of Negativity, but Embrace Positivity

While it's important to be aware of the negative aspects of life, always choose to be part of the positive side. Focus on positivity and let it lead your path.

Law of Attraction

The Law of Attraction asserts that when we embody positivity, the entire universe conspires to support us. Not only does the world align with our goals, but people around us will also collaborate in our success.

Constantly Affirm Positive Thoughts

Words carry magnetic power. Positive words have a unique influence and can shape your life. Transform statements that help your success into powerful affirmations. These will serve as your positive affirmations, reinforcing your mindset.

Magnetic Personality

Positive thoughts have a magnetic quality. They attract not only people but also opportunities and situations that align with your aspirations. Cultivating positivity in your personality creates an environment conducive to success.

Internal Change Is Crucial

External changes are immediately noticeable, but internal changes require more effort and persistence. We must consciously work on improving ourselves from the inside to achieve lasting transformation.

Shift Focus to Good Habits

Success in all areas of life comes from developing positive habits. Work on transforming your mindset and removing negative practices to foster personal growth.

Avoid Negative People

Stay away from individuals who are constantly negative. They will see problems in every solution, draining your energy and focus.

This section emphasizes the power of positivity in shaping our lives. By changing our perspective, nurturing a positive attitude, and constantly focusing on good habits, we can overcome negativity and unlock our full potential. Positivity attracts success, growth, and fulfillment, while negativity can limit our progress.

"If you think you can, you can.

If you think you can't, you can't.

You are right both ways."

- Henry Ford

———————

21.

FROM NARROW-MINDEDNESS TO BROAD-MINDEDNESS

"In the laboratory of humanity,

those who pass the test are the

true human beings."

- Dr. Rajkumar, Actor

Say No to Cramped Thinking

Foster thoughts that reflect greatness. Without compassion, intelligence is futile. Cultivate ideas that expand your mind and heart.

Avoid Inferior Tastes

Enhance your preferences with good habits and meaningful interests. Superior choices contribute to a fulfilling life.

Excessive Selfishness Is Harmful

It's not ideal to always confine yourself to the circle of "me and mine." Broaden your horizons and connect with the larger world.

Perspective for Peace and Achievement

To find contentment, look at those less fortunate than you. To find inspiration, look at those who have achieved greater heights. When you observe those below you, you realize your blessings. When you look up to achievers, you gain clarity about the path you must take.

Universal Brotherhood

Adopt the mindset of "Vasudhaiva Kutumbakam". The world is one family.

- **Participate in Camps**: Involve yourself in activities that bring people together.
- **Join Organizations**: Be part of groups that contribute to society.
- **Engage in Community Work**: Take part in efforts that uplift others.

Avoid a selfish and indifferent attitude. Instead, embrace Kuvempu's vision of a "Universal Human."

Think Global, Act Local

Understand global perspectives and take action in your local environment. The quality of your roots determines the quality of your life. A strong foundation creates a meaningful existence.

The Earth and Its Resources Are Ours

"This earth is mine, this soil is mine, and the water that quenches my thirst belongs to us all." Appreciate and protect the resources that sustain life.

Types of People and Relationships

1. **Emotional Individuals**: They nurture and preserve relationships.
2. **Practical Individuals**: They seek benefits from relationships.
3. **Professional Individuals**: They establish relationships based on profit.

Transform narrow thinking into broad perspectives. By fostering inclusivity, compassion, and higher ideals, we can elevate not just ourselves but also those around us.

—————————

22.

FROM ASSUMPTION TO ADJUSTMENT

"Life is a Garden, Not a Graveyard"

- Sa. Shi. Marulayya

Life is a convergence of many events. It is a series of moments that come together to create our story. This journey is a process of constant adjustments to different situations, and that adaptability is key to a fulfilling life.

Life is a Set of Adjustments

The essence of life lies in the adjustments we make. Life constantly presents us with changes, challenges, and surprises. How we respond to them defines the course of our journey.

Choose the Right Friends

Friendship is vital for a fulfilling life. Choosing the right friends creates an atmosphere of love and support in our lives. The author Prof. L.S. Sheshagiri Rao says, *"When we focus on enemies, we sacrifice our peace."*

Three Types of People

1. **Leaf-like People** (0% contribution)
2. **Branch-like People** (50% contribution)
3. **Tree-like People** (100% contribution)

True happiness is hidden in the happiness of others. When those around us are happy, we too find joy. Respect every drop of water, whether from the sky or the eye.

Sympathy vs. Empathy

Empathy enhances our personality, much more than sympathy. A sense of empathy brings about understanding and deeper connections with others, while sympathy might only be surface-level.

Openness, Closeness, and Perfection

- **Openness** reflects our humility.
- **Closeness** signifies arrogance.
- **Perfection** signifies completeness and maturity.

Doubt, Shame, Honour

While you are on the path of success, there will be doubts. Some may even dishonour you along the way. However, those who truly care will honour you once you achieve your goals. **"Doubt leads to shame, but honour follows achievement."**

Context-Sensitive Behaviour is Key

Behaviour that is appropriate to the context is essential in building trust. Communication and adaptability are closely linked. Instead of focusing on the curiosity of others, it is better to introspect and work on ourselves. Avoid unhelpful criticism, distance yourself from dissatisfied people, and eliminate ego.

Ego Should Go, Positivity Should Grow

- Do not engage in petty conflicts.
- Replace frowning faces with cheerful smiles.
- Do not waste time; help others rise and grow.
- Be aware of misleading minds and attitudes.
- Start with trust and then offer opportunities.
- Ability exceeds intention.
- The people we associate with, and the books we read, shape who we become.
- Adapt to different situations and let your words resonate with positive energy.

Honouring Relationships

- Let sincerity and authenticity be your guides.
- Respect the relationships you nurture and build them with care.
- Cultivate gratitude and kindness to enrich the lives of those around you.

Don't React, Respond

Rather than reacting impulsively, take a moment to reflect and respond thoughtfully. This practice of patience transforms your life. As the saying goes,

"A moment of patience in a moment of anger

saves you a hundred moments of regret."

The Adaptability Quotient

Adaptability is essential for growth. Embrace new experiences, be open to learning, and be willing to make adjustments when things don't go as planned. Continuous exploration and flexibility are key to success.

Embrace the Unexpected

Some people may seem far from us even when physically close. Conversely, some may be physically distant, yet they remain an integral part of our lives. It's important to be clear about who plays what role in our lives, and adjust our behaviour accordingly.

Life is Like Milk

If milk is pure but the container is unclean, it will spoil. Similarly, a pure heart cannot build strong relationships if words and actions are not clean. Even the strongest of bonds will weaken if not nurtured with care.

The Value of Adjusting to Life's Challenges

Life may not always unfold as we expect. However, the real success comes from learning to adapt to challenges. The greater the weight we carry, the harder our journey, but a lighter heart leads to a smoother walk.

"Peace of mind is priceless."

When we leave behind unnecessary burdens and focus on the present, life becomes clearer and more peaceful.

"Don't just chant mantras. When your family is happy,

your home becomes a place of blessings."

- Jayaprakash Nagathihalli

"Stay like a Thread, Not a Cut"

- Namadeva

"Silence preserves relationships.

Excessive silence can break them.

- Jayaprakash Nagathihalli

Conclusion: Embrace Life's Adjustments

Adjustments are central to personal growth and relationships. The ability to adapt with grace, avoid reacting impulsively, and remain calm in the face of challenges makes a huge difference in how we experience life. By developing empathy, humility, and gratitude, we build stronger connections with others and create a fulfilling life for ourselves.

————————

23.

FROM CUSTOMERS TO INVESTORS

"Don't focus on the forest;

look at the tree in front of you."

- Warren Buffett

Equity - Stock Market

As common people, we use a variety of products in our daily lives, from food to vehicles we drive and services provided by banks. By investing in stocks of companies like ITC, Maruti, Tata, Mahindra, Kotak, and Birla, which serve us through their businesses, we can be part of their growth. By either buying shares directly or investing in mutual funds, we can capitalize on India's growing economy and rising population.

Stock Market as a Path to Wealth

Most of the wealthiest individuals in the world have earned their fortunes through the stock market. Stories of individuals like Warren Buffett and Rakesh Jhunjhunwala show the power of investing. If you start investing regularly and stick to a

disciplined approach, you can expect an annual growth rate of about 18%, with the value of your investments multiplying. Sectors such as Information Technology, Pharma, and Banking in India have been showing excellent results.

The Importance of Regular Investment

Start investing early, and make it a habit to invest regularly. Even a small, consistent investment will grow significantly. As the saying goes,

"100 points @ 77,000 points @ with an expected

18% growth every year."

It's important to consult experts or become an expert yourself to make informed decisions.

Inflation and the Need for Investment

Inflation keeps rising every year. If you don't invest your money, its value will continue to diminish. To preserve and grow your wealth, investment is a smart strategy.

Diversify Your Investments

To maintain a balanced investment portfolio, it is crucial to diversify your investments. This means investing in a variety of assets, such as stocks, bonds, and real estate, to reduce risk.

Insurance: A Critical Investment for the Future

Insurance is a vital component of securing your future. Whole life insurance has been popular for years. Today, many private companies offer a range of insurance services. Apart from life insurance, you can also explore health insurance, vehicle insurance, home loans, and more. Take advantage of these services wisely and responsibly.

Gold: The Timeless Investment

Gold has always been a favoured investment option for Indians, and it continues to be attractive due to its rising prices. While women have traditionally been the primary investors in gold, more men are now seeing the benefits of investing in yellow metal.

Real Estate: A Steady Investment Avenue

Real estate is a powerful investment, particularly in urban areas where property prices are rising rapidly. However, it is essential to gather complete information and be cautious before making investments. Real estate investments include not just plots but also apartments and villas. Many wealthy people today flaunt their homes as symbols of prosperity.

Post Office: Government-Supported Schemes

The Post Office offers various investment opportunities, including National Savings Certificates, bonds, and fixed deposits. These schemes provide a secure option for long-term savings. Be sure to gather detailed information before proceeding.

Banks and Fixed Deposits

With the advent of private banks competing alongside Nationalized ones, banking services have become more accessible. Banks also offer fixed deposits (FDs) with different schemes that suit various financial goals. Research the available options and invest wisely.

Co-operative Banks

Co-operative banks are a growing option in India, providing tailored services to communities. However, be cautious with co-operative banks as some may have issues, so it's essential to choose reliable ones.

Mutual Funds

Systematic Investment Plans (SIP) are becoming a popular and disciplined way to invest. This method allows you to invest regularly in mutual funds, helping you to build wealth. It's also flexible, allowing you to withdraw funds if needed in emergencies.

Chit Funds

Chit funds are another option where people contribute to a pooled fund, often used for emergencies. While some of these schemes have been strengthened legally, it is still important to be cautious and invest in trusted companies. Avoid getting involved in personal chit funds run by individuals unless you have full trust in their credibility.

Business: High Earning Potential

Business is often the most lucrative way to make money. If you are passionate about a specific business, investing in it can yield significant returns. Many investors recognize profitable businesses and fund their ventures, with many achieving great success.

Entrepreneurship: A Path to Financial Freedom

Starting your own business and managing your capital is one of the most rewarding paths to wealth. Entrepreneurship allows you to be in control of your financial future and is an exciting journey of growth and self-discovery.

Skills are Your Greatest Assets

Investing in developing your skills can greatly increase your earning potential. By focusing on improving your skills, you can grow your wealth. Always invest in learning, as this will benefit you throughout your life.

Investing in Yourself: The Best Investment

The greatest investment you can make is in yourself. Investing in your knowledge, skills, mindset, and habits will yield the highest returns. As the saying goes, *"An investment in yourself is the best investment you can make."* Seek out mentors and learning opportunities that will help you grow personally and professionally.

Books on Money Management

There are many excellent books on managing money and investing wisely. By reading these books, you can improve your financial knowledge and work towards achieving wealth.

Conclusion: Results Matter

As Rakesh Jhunjhunwala famously says,

"Your results are what matter the most."

Focus on consistent, smart investment decisions, diversify your portfolio, and always keep learning to build your wealth.

———————————-

24.

ARTICLES TO BOOKS

The signature changes your writing.

Believe in this statement.

You can shape your life.

YOU CAN SCRIPT YOUR OWN FUTURE

Importance of Writing

It is an important aspect of communication. Your writing is equivalent to a record. It has a solid and influential personality. You should use this aspect with understanding. This is a solution to many of your problems.

The pen is mightier than the sword.

The history of the world has proven this fact. Even today, and forever, this remains an influential aspect.

Writing Therapy

Recently, writing is being used as a therapy for mental satisfaction.

One BOOK

One PEN

One CHILD

One TEACHER

Can CHANGE THE WORLD

Content Writing

BE A CONTENT CREATOR, NOT A CONSUMER.

CONTENT WRITING HAS BECOME THE #1 SKILL.

Copywriting
Writing for promotion brings in more money.

Turn Your Words Into Money

The Importance of Words

Those who are rich in words become achievers.

- Readers Digest

- Research *on Vocabulary*

- Do not make mistakes in usage.

- Give life to words.

- Language development through sentence construction.

Positive Affirmations

Auto Suggestions

WANTED – UNWANTED

"If drops of honey meet, they form a pit,
If drops of water meet, they form a stream."

Roles in Writing:

One who writes articles is a **WRITER.**

One who writes books is an **AUTHOR.**

One who writes editorials is an **EDITOR.**

One who writes notes is a **TEACHER.**

One who writes destiny is a **CREATOR.**

Activities:

- Adopt the habit of pen and paper.

- Collect your thoughts by writing a journal.

- Make writing your daily practice.

- Create books from your thoughts.

- Your responses on social media can improve your writing.

[COMMENTING ON SOCIAL MEDIA IMPROVES YOUR LANGUAGE]

May the ink of the great writer's pen
Never end as long as his life continues.

- Justice Shivraj Patil

————————

25.

RECEIVING TO GIVING

"The cloth worn by a dead

Does not have pockets."

- Alexander

When you give, the growth is more.

When I spoke to several rich people, they said that as much as we give in charity, our money keeps growing. If unknown people still remember you, it means that at a time when they had no one; you did something for them that was needed.

Generosity - Giving in your circumstances

Even when one does not have enough, those with a giving mindset continue to give.

Start by sharing knowledge

You can only share what you have. If you have knowledge, start from there.

We receive from nature

We must plant trees. Under no circumstances should we destroy the environment. If there is a reason, we should protect nature. A model example of this is the story of Salumarada Thimmakka, who had no children but cared for thousands of trees, treating them like her children.

Self-reliance - IMPORT TO EXPORT

India was once a country that imported many goods. Now it has grown to a level where it exports many goods. This example is shared to highlight how giving leads to progress in all areas.

Help others by extending your hand

We can help those around us in need. By using such moments, we become better human beings.

No person in this world has ever been rewarded for what he has RECEIVED.

He is always honoured for what he has GIVEN to others.

Do you have an SB Account?

Do you have a Current Account?

Do you have a GIVING Account?

"The person who lives only for himself

will not be remembered in this world."

"The person who lives for others will never be forgotten."

"Rivers do not drink their own water."

"Trees do not eat their own fruits.'

"Rain and clouds do not eat the crops."

Questionnaire:

Q. When to give?

A. Now.

Q. How much?

A. As much as you can give.

Q. What?

A. A flower, a smile, a back support, a hand.

Q. To whom?

A. To those who need it.

Q. How?

A. Give without expectations.

"The more you give, the more you receive."

Saint Kabir says:

"When wealth increases at home,

When water fills the boat,

Use both hands to throw it away."

Experience from the Buddhist Temple:

At a Buddhist temple, no matter how much we gave, they would always take 100 coins. When inquired, they said that the practice was to keep the boxes and continue this practice 100 times. This helps in cultivating the habit of giving.

"Life smiles at you when you are happy,
But life salutes when you make others happy."

———————-

26.

EMPLOYMENT TO ENTREPRENEURSHIP

Essential aspects for most people in the initial phase of employment

In the book ***"Employability Skills"***, details are provided on how to get a job and how to find happiness in the workplace. While in employment, keep these aspects in mind:

"Have a friendly attitude with your peers."

"Show respect to those older than you."

"Maintain humanity with your juniors."

- Jayaprakash Nagathihalli

Entrepreneurship - The need of today

Many people have the mindset that education is for securing a job. Some professional courses even offer placement facilities, which attract students. Even students of business-related courses are joining colleges that offer placements. This might be fine in the initial stages, but the author's intention is to encourage you to strive to become an entrepreneur eventually.

Entrepreneurs are needed in all sectors

Entrepreneurs are needed in almost all sectors of the country. Countries with more entrepreneurs are the ones that are more developed.

Employers are considered superior

If you are an employer, your employees will view you like a god. They will worship you.

Creativity in entrepreneurship

In entrepreneurship, there is a greater degree of creativity. We become our own bosses. We are always inclined towards development. There is a constant desire to outdo others. Hence, the level of creativity is much higher.

Entrepreneurship makes you more proactive

Being active like a foot soldier is an essential characteristic.

Be Your Own Boss

We stand on our own feet and form teams to become leaders.

Identify the field you wish to do business in

Engage more and more in the field you wish to enter for business. This will help you later.

Get training and perform

Get as much training as possible in the field you want to be recognized in and perform accordingly.

Entrepreneurs and online platforms

Due to the growth of technology, online platforms are a boon today. Social media can also support you. Use it properly.

Good relationships are the foundation for good business

Build strong relationships with more people. *"Network is Net worth"* is a proven truth.

Qualities of Entrepreneurs

1. Dreamer - Recognition
2. Curiosity
3. Flexibility (like iron and wood)
4. Patience
5. Willingness to take risks

Positive developments

- Entrepreneurial universities are starting.
- Management institutes are offering incubation opportunities.
- Private organizations are responding to new ideas.
- Clubs related to entrepreneurship are starting.
- Events that encourage entrepreneurship are increasing.
- Business plan competitions are inspiring youth.
- Technological developments are complementing this trend.
- The youth is also responding.

————————-

27.

LEADERSHIP TO
TEAM BUILDER

ANT

"I will approach the sweetness of the sugar,

And bring the good news, gathering the group.

I will carry one burden at a time,

And return after completing my task.

Together, in a line, the army moves forward,

I will gather food during the monsoon season.

I will be cautious and wise,

And give advice to be an employee."

- V.C. Irsang

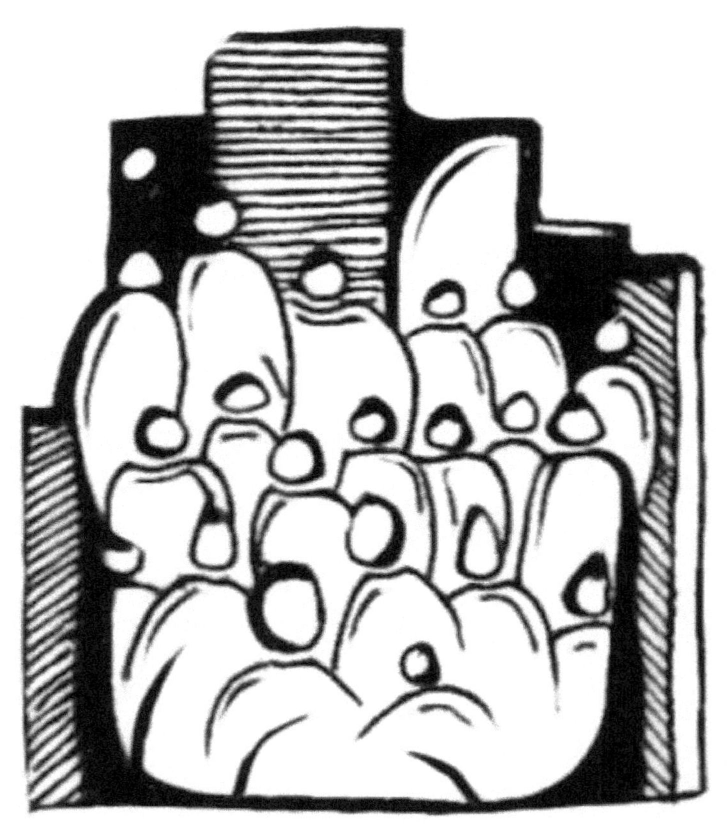

Start acting like a leader

We must act as we want to become. Many times, we unknowingly reach our goal by following this principle.

Understand leadership qualities

Understand the life of a leader. Recognize their qualities and behaviours. Identify which aspects help you and then adopt them.

Use 'We' instead of 'I'

Changing the mindset of everything was possible for me. When you say, "We all made it happen," everyone will be more willing to join you.

Exhibit a 'leader within you' attitude

When you convey the message of "I am a leader among you" through your words and actions, your team will stand strong with you.

Assign the right responsibility to the right person

Identifying the strengths of team members is a leader's important task. Assigning the right responsibility to the right person ensures half of the success is already achieved.

Say 'When we lost, it was my loss; when we won, it was because of all of us'

When the team loses, say,

"Our loss." When they win, acknowledge,

"It was because of all of you."

Engage in organizations to be socially active

Organizations help in recognizing you within the mainstream of society. Align yourself with the right organizations.

NETWORK IS NET WORTH

The value of an individual is determined by the number of connections they have.

A leader is the reflection of the group

If you represent a group, you also represent their qualities.

Example:

Look at the factors that contributed to India's success in the 2024 T20 World Cup:

- Playing for the team, not just for records.
- Excellence in batting, bowling, and fielding.
- Rahul Dravid's guidance.
- Rohit Sharma's leadership.
- Veteran player Virat Kohli's experience.
- All bowlers put in an excellent effort.

Focusing on the leadership qualities, the importance of teamwork, and the approach to building and leading a successful team.

TEAM

T – Together

E – Everyone

A – Achieves

M – More

____

28.

ACTIVITIES TO ACTION-ORIENTED

Wonderful Works

Your continuous small acts of service form a beautiful collection.

First Step Syndrome

Why hesitate to take the first step? Many people lose out on huge opportunities in life simply by delaying the first step. By not acting, they miss out on tremendous growth.

Good Habits are Like a Lifeline

From a young age, we must cultivate good habits. Engaging in creative activities makes us mentally and physically stronger. Our artistic skills contribute significantly to this.

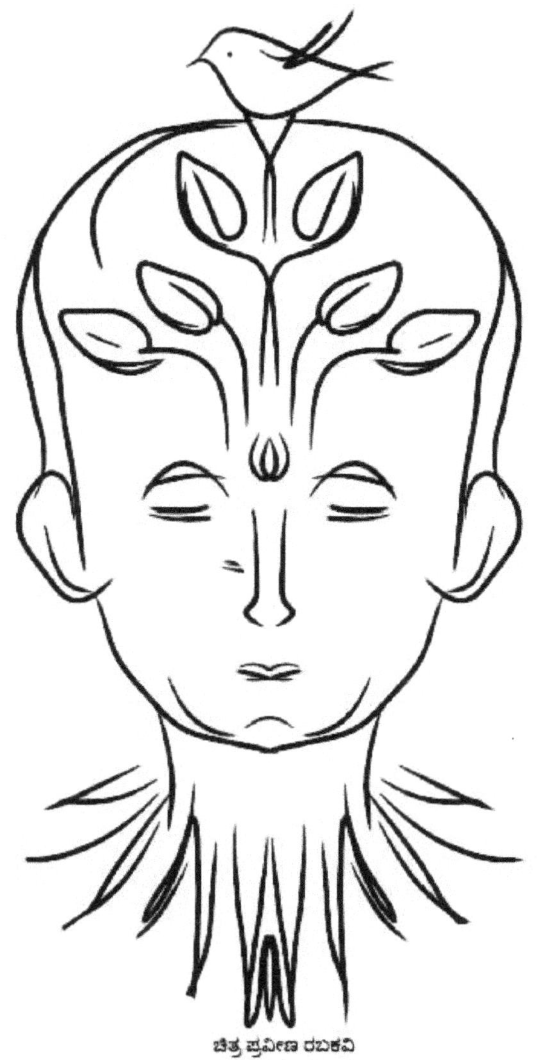

ಚಿತ್ರ ಪ್ರವೀಣ ರಬಕವಿ

Hobbies Shape; Habits Shine

Hobbies brighten our lives. Our habits shape our personality and play a crucial role in making us good citizens.

Action Cures Fear

Fear often prevents us from experiencing life fully. Your proactive activities build the path to success.

Make a List of Your Dreams, Underline the Big Dreams

Take leadership in the field you represent. Build strong friendships with your team members.

Roots Create Fruits

As good as your learning, as sweet will be its outcome. The more dissatisfied we are with our learning, the better. Many people are stuck in contentment and fail to grow further.

Small Corrections Make Big Impact

We must make changes in our lives. These corrections can take us to the peak of success.

Activities Suggested by JP:

- Write down your thoughts in a Journal.

- Keep a daily record of your activities.

- Practice making a checklist of tasks you need to complete.

- If you were to write your autobiography, imagine how the plot would unfold. This helps form a clear picture of your life.

- Create a Vision Board with your dreams as goals and visualize them.

- Write positive affirmations and place them where you can see them daily.

- Listen to audio of positive thoughts regularly.

- Watch videos related to personal development and comment on them. [For example: Jayaprakash Nagathihalli and Transformation Unlimited YouTube channels]

- Read motivational and transformative books. [Read all works by the author in this regard.]

- Participate in both ONLINE & OFFLINE training sessions.

- Seek guidance from excellent mentors.

- Engage in physical activities.

- Yoga and meditation are excellent methods.

- Build good relationships with your family, neighbours, friends, and colleagues.

- Focus on financial matters and start learning income-generating skills.

- Pay special attention to finances, earn, save, and grow.

- Actively participate in any competitions you wish to.

- Extracurricular activities contribute to the development of your personality.

- Public speaking courses boost self-confidence.

- Personality development camps foster leadership growth.

Select Your Activities Wisely

Over time, harmful and aimless habits can sneak into your lifestyle. When you identify them and make changes, those habits present great opportunities for improvement. Eliminate unnecessary and negative activities and make room for better, useful ones. Recognize activities that waste your time and challenge yourself to replace them.

Focus on positive change that excites and motivates you. By utilizing your time, energy, and resources effectively, you reward yourself with true and attractive rewards.

When your choices improve, your results improve. Add richness to your life through positive and encouraging actions every day.

You have the power to discern what you should do and what you should avoid. Apply this understanding to guide your choices and inspire your actions.

Leave behind aimless, peace-destroying habits, and return to activities that are full of enthusiasm and bring prosperity.

Be mindful in selecting your activities, ensuring they enhance the value they bring to your life.

Look for activities that waste your time, energy, and effort. Identify them and change them appropriately to increase your value.

UPDATE OR BE OUTDATED

This translation focuses on the importance of moving from passive activities to proactive, action-oriented choices, incorporating wisdom about habits, self-improvement, and making the most of one's time and energy for greater personal growth.

"Small joys are the baskets of happiness."

––––––––

29.

SUCCESS PATH TO TOPPER

Two-Wheeler to Train Track

Two-wheeler drivers move here and there, but trains run only on tracks. Similarly, we need to bring our tasks onto a clear track, much like a train follows its path.

Movement to Fly

Continuous momentum keeps pushing you forward. Eventually, with persistence, you will be able to soar and fly.

Consistent Practice Leads to Success

The desire to grow will elevate you. How high you rise depends on you. If you have the opportunity to choose, always pick the best option. If you don't have a choice, do what you can with excellence.

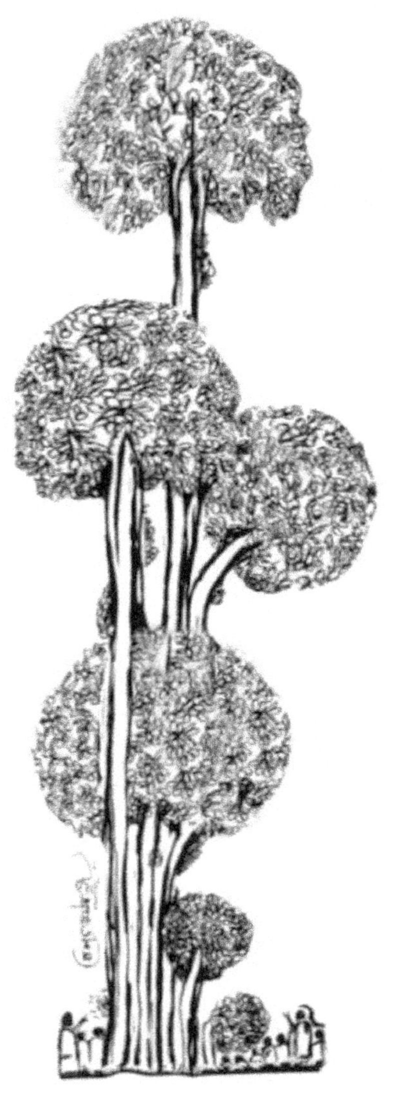

Achieving Results

Only those who work diligently and consistently can attain success. May such efforts be yours.

Recognize Yourself as a Professional

In cricket, many players became professionals because they dedicated themselves fully. For example, Sunil Gavaskar, Sachin Tendulkar, and Dhoni. By maintaining professionalism and respect for your field, you too can become a successful achiever.

Read the Biographies of Successful People

The life stories of successful individuals serve as guiding lights. The author has interviewed 2000 successful people, gaining invaluable experience. About 400 of these interviews are available in videos on the Jayaprakash Nagathihalli and Transformation Unlimited YouTube channels, where readers can gain insights.

Adopt the Qualities of Successful People

Each successful person possesses unique qualities. We must recognize how these qualities can benefit us and adopt them.

Increase Your Influence

By identifying your uniqueness and continuously developing your skills, your influence will grow as well.

Become a Success Yourself

By observing other successful people, you can also achieve success. We must continuously adopt the good qualities of others.

Continue as a Successful Person

It's not enough to just be considered successful once. You must carry forward the legacy of that success, continuing to work hard. This way, you will solidify your position in your field.

This translation emphasizes the importance of consistent effort, recognizing professional qualities, and learning from the lives of successful individuals to become a top achiever. It encourages persistence and continual growth, both in skills and character, in order to reach and maintain success.

————————

30.

SLOW TO FAST

Slow and Steady Wins the Race

We often hear these phrases:

"Speed thrills but kills,"

and

"Competition is not always good"

Slow pace can be beneficial in certain situations, but it can also hinder major progress. This text aims to draw your attention to the importance of speed in some areas.

Air Travel

Unlike other forms of transport, planes allow for faster travel. Today, supersonic planes are capable of moving at incredibly high speeds. Similarly, the bullet train has been built for speed. In the modern age, we see a growing preference for speed.

Speed Reading

Recently, speed reading has gained popularity. Many individuals now offer training in this technique. By learning speed reading, you can quickly consume books and gain knowledge.

Do Today What You Can Do Tomorrow

Procrastination is the cause of many of our problems. If we complete tasks today, we can avoid many future issues.

The Story of the Tortoise and the Hare

Everyone is familiar with the story where the slow-moving tortoise eventually wins the race against the speedy hare. However, in another race, the hare wins because it races with speed. In a third race, the tortoise invites the hare to race in a mixed terrain, where the tortoise is faster in the water and the hare on land. Both win, illustrating how a combination of speed and strategy leads to success. This mindset should be cultivated by all of us.

Acceleration - The 10X Rule

Love speed. We wish for personal growth, not for regression. Never settle for less. Take control of all elements that contribute to your life. Expand your goals 10X, increase your efforts by 10X, and success will follow. Start making decisions quickly. Speed leads to speed. Master your speed, increase your focus, and be action-oriented. Pay attention to current trends.

Combination of Slow and Fast

The right balance of speed and patience can be helpful to everyone. Just like a vehicle's speed depends on its driver and its capability, we must identify the right pace for our life. Sometimes, patience and perseverance help us control our mind.

Pause when necessary.

"It does not matter how slowly you go,

as long as you do not stop."

- Confucius

A balance between slow and fast approaches in life. While slow, steady progress is important, speed and decisiveness are necessary to achieve greater success. The text encourages mastering one's pace, learning new skills (like speed reading), and balancing patience with action for continuous growth and achievement.

Clock

The clock is like a lion, tirelessly turning without rest. If it stops, it will face reproach. It measures time with its rotating hands, without caring for quiet times or revolutionary moments. You keep going, without concern for the criticism, and your patience becomes your strength.

- V.C. Irsang

————————-

31.

MENTORING TO SCALING UP

Knowledge

To receive mentorship, one must be like a mute and a joker, as explained by the philosopher Kadikoala Madiwalaeshwara. The teaching goes:

- Be mute in this world
- Be like a joker
- Learn to speak
- Understand the essence of words
- Even a great scholar must stay close to the wise.
- Learn the philosophy
- Understand the meaning of the philosophy
- Even a scholar of philosophy must stay close to the wise
- Have desire and sincerity
- Cleanse your mind of all confusion

Guru (Mentor)

A guru's guidance leads us to greatness. You must adopt the mindset of total surrender to learning. A true mentor shows the path towards knowledge.

Direction – Compass

"The clock shows the time,

but *the compass shows the direction.*"

"The importance of guidance arises

when learning takes priority."

"Once the direction is set,

time management becomes important."

Mirror Principle

As the reflection in the mirror reveals, guidance involves showing the way to others. A mentor's role is wide-ranging and crucial. The guidance leads to success by lighting the path of knowledge and inspiration.

Learning Partners

Those who seek knowledge and those who guide are partners in learning. The mentor creates a solid foundation for learning.

Continuous training and development generate an environment where change and transformation are encouraged.

Fast Learning through Mentorship

With the help of a good mentor, learning can be fast-tracked. A mentor accelerates your growth.

"Mentor is a catalyst."

Those Who Have Learned Well Can Guide Well

A true mentor learns first and then guides others. This method creates a thriving and harmonious society.

7 Types of Learning

1. Lecture – 5%

2. Reading – 10%

3. Listening & Watching – 20%

4. Demonstration – 30%

5. Group Discussion – 50%

6. Practice through Doing – 75%

7. Teaching Others – 90%

[Learn Do Teach]

Patience is Key

Those who lack patience for learning are not ready for greatness. As the proverb says, climbing the tree may turn the head, and wealth may cloud one's wisdom.

Every Profession Grows Through Mentorship

Every field advances with the guidance of experts. We should acknowledge the experts in every domain and cultivate a generation that desires to learn from them. Schools and colleges must provide quality mentorship for this purpose.

Different Forms of Guidance

- **Teacher** (Teaching)
- **Trainer** (Training)
- **Coach** (Coaching)
- **Counsellor** (Counselling)
- **Consultant** (Consulting)

These roles emerge from the need for guidance in various forms.

How to Scale Up?

- **UPDATE**: Keep renewing.
- **UPGRADE**: Rise higher.
- **BEST VERSION**: Transform into your best self.
- **RE-INVENT**: Rediscover yourself.
- **RE-WIRING**: Embrace new paths.
- **RE-POSITIONING**: Re-establish yourself.
- **RE-VISIT**: Revisit your goals.
- **RE-CHARGE**: Refill your energy.
- **CHANNELISE**: Direct yourself properly.
- **BE UNIQUE**: Be one of a kind.
- **BE A NEW YOU**: Transform into a new version of yourself.
- **BE A PLAYER**: Be an active participant.
- **BEAT YOURSELF**: Challenge yourself to grow.
- **TREASURE HOUSE**: Be a treasure chest of knowledge.
- **POWER HOUSE**: Be a powerhouse of energy.
- **MASTERPIECE**: Be a masterpiece.
- **BECOME CEO OF YOUR LIFE**: Be the CEO of your life.
- **SCRIPT YOUR FUTURE**: Create your own future.
- **DISCOVER THE DIAMOND IN YOU**: Uncover the potential within you.
- **TUNE & FINE-TUNE**: Refine yourself.
- **POLISHING**: Shine brighter.
- **ENHANCE**: Enhance your capabilities.
- **STEP UP**: Take action.
- **LIFT UP**: Lift yourself higher.
- **ELEVATE**: Raise yourself to new heights.
- **BE AN EXPERT**: Become an expert.

- **BECOME A LEGEND**: Become legendary.
- **CONNECTING THE DOTS**: Connecting experiences and knowledge.
- **LAUNCHING PAD**: Be the launch pad for your success.
- **LLL - LifeLong Learner Approach**: Keep learning throughout life.

Quotes on Mentorship

"Mentoring is a brain to pick, an ear to listen and

a push in the right direction."

- John C. Crosby

"The delicate balance of mentoring someone is not

creating them in your own image,

but giving them the opportunity to create themselves."

- Steven Spielberg

"A Mentor is someone who allows you to

see the hope inside yourself."

- Oprah Winfrey

"A Mentor is someone who sees more talent and ability within you, than you see in yourself, and helps bring it out of you."

- Bob Proctor

"Every great achiever is inspired by a great mentor."

- Laila Gifty Akita

"One of the greatest values of mentors is the ability to see ahead what others cannot see and to help t hem navigate a course to their destination."

- John C. Maxwell

"The personal one-on-one aspect of MENTORING is something our society desperately needs."

- Tony Dungy

"A good coach can change a game.

A great coach can change a life."

- John Wooden

Growth Through Deep Roots

To grow a tree tall, its roots must go deep into the ground. Similarly, to grow in life, we must develop gratitude and compassion, deeply rooted in our hearts.

Everyday is a New Challenge

Every day is an opportunity to fly high. Until you spread your wings, you have no idea how high you can go.

This text emphasizes the importance of mentorship, continual learning, and personal growth. It encourages individuals to seek guidance from experts, embrace mentorship, and scale up their potential through updated learning strategies and consistent efforts. It also highlights the diverse ways mentorship can manifest (teaching, coaching, counselling, etc.), and the mindset needed to grow and transform in life.

———————

32.

WANDER TO WONDER-STRUCK

Nomadic Life Settlement

- Strength, time, and effort
- Achievement is difficult at high speeds.

TWO WHEELER TO RAILWAY TRACK

- First the track, then the ascent.

Advantages of Settling Down

- Progress
- Experience
- Wealth
- Knowledge

Wow! You must be looked at with wonder

- Satisfaction
- Progress practically â€" *Be Practical*
- Focus: Instead of spreading efforts thin, focus on one target

Travel the Country, Read Books

- Adapt and push forward.
- Read the biographies of achievers.
- Measuring Stick - Holistic Approach (Comprehensive Integration)

This text encourages transitioning from a wandering life to a more focused, purposeful one. It emphasizes the importance of grounding oneself, making steady progress, and focusing on practical, meaningful goals. It also calls for the pursuit of knowledge, reading, and learning from achievers, while striving for a holistic and well-rounded growth.

—————————

33.

ORDINARY TO EXTRAORDINARY

"Everyone who achieved Fame

were once ordinary individuals."

- Jayaprakash Nagathihalli

The purpose of life is to grow and transform. Choices directly influence the journey of our life. Our biology helps us move forward. Just as cells create a new life, the harmony between the brain and nervous system creates quantum leaps in our lives. We understand our surroundings through our nervous system.

BIOLOGICAL QUANTUM LEAP

- The body activates through the production of serotonin, dopamine, and endorphins.
- Oxytocin causes a 200x flow of energy, rapidly stopping anger.

- Despite challenges, experiences in life help unify our growth.

Take Risks

- Becoming extraordinary is about surpassing the ordinary. It means overcoming barriers to reach higher understanding.
- *"Hardships often prepare ordinary people for an extraordinary destiny."* - C.S. Lewis

You Are the Leader of Your Life

- Be the real hero of your life, not a reel (fictional) hero.
- Recognize your uniqueness and difference.
- You are the masterpiece of your own life.
- You are the sculptor of your own success.

The Power of EXTRA

Adding *Extra* before ordinary makes the difference:

- Extra - Ordinary
- Extra - Mile
- Extra - Effort
- Extra - Smile
- Extra - Excellence
- Extra - Efficiency
- Extra - Energy

- Extra - Elasticity
- Extra - YOU

Even a 1% improvement can take you to the top.

- Stretch like a rubber band.

D.V.G.'s Poem:

"The world is as large as your eyes, ears, and mind can perceive. Whatever makes you cry or laugh, is within you. When you grow beyond these limitations, your world will expand, and you will outgrow 'small-mindedness."
Mankutimma

True Achievement

- True success is not when those who rejected us turn away, but when they are forced to look back at us in admiration.

Reflection

"Living blindly, not knowing what's ahead, and thinking

that today's needs are enough is the wrong mindset."

-V.C. Irsang

Activity:

- Understand your uniqueness.
- Read and reflect on works that inspire growth.

This piece emphasizes the transformation from an ordinary life to an extraordinary one through growth, embracing challenges, and recognizing one's unique power. It encourages a mindset of progress and expansion, where each small improvement can bring significant results.

————————-

34.

LOVE TO GOD

How Can a Flower Bloom Without Love?

How can a cloud form without love?

How can the dew fall and bring greenery without love?

-G.S. Shivrudrappa

What is love?

- It is a verb (an action), a noun (a concept), a universal truth, and an ideal.
- It is the common thread in all religions, a path, a psychological event, and an experience.
- It is a feeling that creates a deep connection. It can even be a biochemical reaction.
- Love is the essence of life - *B.R. Lakshmanarao.*
- In the middle of actions, there lies a message.
- Ask yourself: Define your own understanding of love.

Tibetan Proverb:

"The secret to living well and longer is: eat half, walk double, laugh triple, and love without measure."

Love Life

- True love for life begins with self-love.
- Understanding your own value is essential.
- You are a masterpiece; accept and appreciate yourself.
- Love people, use things.

Unconditional Love

"The unconditional aspect of love changes the world."

-Sage Robbins

Elements of Love

- **Forgiveness**: Love and forgive others.
- **Love as a Path to the Divine**: Love is a bridge to higher understanding, just as a journey to Jyotirlinga (sacred place) is.
- Don't dwell on mistakes, but forgive yourself.
- Trust yourself and know your beauty.
- Live according to your choices.
- Love creates connections and strengthens relationships.

Ways to Foster a Loving Environment

- **Satsang (spiritual gatherings)**
- **Environment**: Surround yourself with positivity.
- **Guru**: Seek wisdom and guidance.
- **Food, Lifestyle, Conversations, Travel**: Maintain a healthy, mindful approach.
- **Books**: Enrich your mind with knowledge.
- Move from darkness to light through wisdom.
- **The teacher who imparts knowledge is a Guru -** *Sage*.
- **Passion for Life**: Enthusiasm brings joy and purpose.

Love is a Universal Language

- For everything else, love is enough.
- Love is understood by everyone, including children and even animals.

Love in Action

- When the lamp of love is lit, it automatically opens the door of the heart.
- The light of love leads to the growth and elevation of life.
- Spiritual growth and self-elevation are intertwined with love.

Charlie Chaplin's Wisdom

"You need power only when you want to do something harmful; otherwise, love is enough to get everything done."

Love and the Divine

"Love is God; God is love."

"Love transcends all boundaries and limitations."

This message emphasizes the power and transformative force of love, not just in human relationships but also in spiritual connection. It encourages self-love, forgiveness, and the importance of creating a loving environment for personal and collective growth.

———–

35.

EGO TO PROUDNESS

"Success that is achieved after a long struggle shapes one's personality. Immediate success creates arrogance."

-Sudha Murthy

Those who are full of ego are not necessarily great individuals.

- When observing the lives of achievers, some with ego may be successful, but they are not necessarily considered great individuals.

There is a fine line between ego and pride:

- Ego, when it exceeds limits, can harm both the individual and others around them. It is essential to correct this when it becomes disruptive.

Pride always brings a Sense of Honour.

- When our behaviour complements our pride, it generates positive feelings. Pride enhances our self-respect.

The word "I" has one meaning, but the feelings it evokes are many.

- Although the meaning of "I" is singular, its associated feelings are diverse. When we speak with pride and exhibit it through our behaviour, it does not harm anyone.

Pride brings a sense of happiness and contentment:

- Pride instills a sense of joy and contentment in us, brightening our lives. Pride helps lead us toward positivity.
- It is crucial to have pride in ourselves first, before looking for it in others. Embracing pride in oneself builds inner strength and stability.

Pride - an experience.

- Govindaraj, a person we encountered, was passionate about the way we conduct ourselves. He would consistently come to the hotel where we were training and help us arrange all the materials. On one occasion, he asked us to send our two boys, Pavan and Naveen, to serve as volunteers for a workshop. When they came to us and says, **"Our father, JP Sir, said you must polish shoes,"** we were moved.

- Such positive experiences reveal that pride can motivate and lead to transformation. It is our hope that everyone will embrace pride and move toward personal growth and positive change.

Albert Einstein's Wisdom

"There is a direct connection between knowledge and arrogance.
The less knowledge one has, the greater the arrogance."

———————-

36.

TRANSFORMATION TO ACHIEVER

"We must constantly strive to refine our lives.
A life that is not tested is not truly a life."

-Socrates, Greek Philosopher

Mankutimma's Kagga:

"Are you waiting for the adornment of your virtues,

or are you focusing on your true qualities?

Leaving behind the adornment,

is it the animal's work?"

- Mankutimma (Verse 213)

Just as animals, birds, and insects do not leave their inherent qualities, humans too should not neglect their negative traits or see them as natural. As knowledge comes, humans strive to correct their unnatural qualities, and by doing so, they bring order to their lives. This constant effort is the path of evolution.

Compared to all other creatures, humans are gifted with the ability to think critically. By overcoming negative traits, a human can be recognized as a civilized person. Yet, some remain stuck in basic, animal-like tendencies, indicating they have not yet transcended animal instincts. A life of humanity surpasses an animal's existence, and a divine life exceeds that of humanity. Ultimately, divine life is the goal, and humans are meant to evolve towards this state, as per divine order.

The Six Dimensions of Personality:

1. Physical Personality
2. Mental Personality
3. Intellectual Personality
4. Emotional Personality
5. Spiritual Personality
6. Economic Personality

You are the driver of a vehicle with six wheels. Shape your future.

Key Principles for Becoming an Achiever:

- Become a member of the 1% club for excellence.

- Know who you are, where you are, and where you want to go.
- Live a simple life with lofty thoughts.
- Reinvent yourself and rise to the next level.
- Multi-dimensional growth.
- Six Sigma: Zero defects.
- Consistency and gradual effort bring lasting results.

Levels of Success:

- Position, wealth, power, and knowledge are critical stages.
- A desire for superheroes often arises from the frustration of our own limitations.
- Control your shadows: selfishness, greed, hunger, jealousy, anger, and desire.
- Develop virtues: greatness, compassion, gratitude, forgiveness, courage, and love for others.

Consistency

- Even marginal improvement can create a huge impact.

Control the negative traits such as selfishness, jealousy, hunger, envy, and anger.

- Follow the framework of virtues: greatness, compassion, gratitude, forgiveness, patience, and love for others.

Contentment and Achievement:

- To feel content, compare yourself with those who are less fortunate than you.
- For achieving great things, look to those who have achieved more and strive to be like them.

Intense Pursuit Leads to Greater Heights:

- Galileo's curiosity led him to become an astronomer and mathematician, explaining the Earth's motion.
- Edmund Hillary, when initially unable to conquer Everest, says, "I will come again, I will climb you. You may not grow, but I will. I will keep climbing."

Growth Beyond Limits:

- Words like "No change is possible" are often used by those who resist growth, but environments and circumstances can change anyone.
- Remember, the outlaw Valmiki became the revered sage, symbolizing the power of transformation.

Internal vs. External Factors:

- Internal growth comes from within, while external factors include how others see us.
- Introverts and Extroverts differ in their approach to the world.

- Involvement leads to evolution.
- Hard work versus smart work: there's value in both, but one should focus on using intelligence wisely.

Luck vs. Action:

- True progress comes from action, not mere hope.
- Optimism versus pessimism: an optimistic outlook will always guide us toward success.

The Path to Success:

- Start with the end in mind and move forward with clarity.
- Familiarity breeds confidence: The more familiar you are with a task, the more confident you become.

Imperfection is Perfect:

- Waiting for perfection is a mistake. Achievements are born from efforts at every stage of life.
- Being effort-driven from the beginning is key to success.

Shortcuts Will Cut You Short:

- Don't opt for shortcuts; they often lead to incomplete achievements.

Mend or End:

- If you don't adapt to change, you risk facing a dead-end in life.

"Positive Change is Transformation"

Respect Life, Respect the Living:

"Life is a journey of growth and transformation,

and we must honour its process."

-*Mankuthimma's Vachana (475)*

This profound section emphasizes the importance of continuous improvement, introspection, and discipline to move from transformation to achievement. It encourages personal growth across various dimensions and emphasizes consistency, hard work, and a positive attitude in achieving success.

———————-

37.

JP AT JOSH TALKS ABOUT LIFE AND TRANSFORMATION

Jayaprakash Nagathihalli's journey and transformation in life is deeply inspiring, especially his emphasis on personal development, continuous learning, and overcoming challenges. His story highlights the importance of confidence, perseverance, and embracing opportunities, even if they seem daunting at first.

He starts by sharing how he faced challenges when he moved to Bangalore in the fifth grade, where his classmates spoke English fluently, and how he struggled with the language. Despite the ridicule he faced for speaking differently, his teacher encouraged him to focus on his studies and ignore the negative comments. his advice helped him succeed and earn the second rank in a test, proving that staying focused on personal growth can overcome external judgments.

He also reflects on his varied educational journey, from pursuing science, arts, and commerce to completing a diploma in journalism and later working in mass communication. His story stresses that a multi-disciplinary approach can help build a balanced perspective, and continuous learning is crucial for success.

EMPOWERING
YOUTH AND ENTREPRENEURS
DIGITAL MARKETING SKILLS
KS
Make
it
happen

Another key aspect of his transformation was his involvement in extracurricular activities. He believes that true success comes not only from academic achievements but also from engaging in activities that nurture personal skills, such as public speaking, debating, and leadership roles. This hands-on experience, according to him, can shape one's personality and help them stand out in their professional life.

Jayaprakash also shares how his journey in communication began with a radio program, where he overcame his shyness and improved his language skills. His passion for public speaking eventually led him to become a newsreader and a trainer, impacting thousands of individuals through motivational speeches and training programs. He emphasizes that personal growth comes from taking risks and making an effort to improve, even if it means facing failure along the way.

One of his most powerful messages is about the importance of believing in oneself and taking action. He talks about the impact of his role as a mentor and how he helped students realize their potential. Through his organization, Nagamma Foundation, he has been able to empower students by boosting their self-confidence and helping them overcome feelings of inferiority.

His story culminates with the emotional tribute to his mother, who passed away unexpectedly. He turned his grief into motivation by starting the Nagamma Foundation, ensuring that her name lives on and continues to inspire others. Jayaprakash's message is clear: no matter the hardships, we have the power to transform ourselves and contribute positively to the world around us. His story is a testament to the fact that through continuous learning, determination, and self-belief, we can overcome any challenge and make a lasting impact on others.

In essence, Jayaprakash's life is a lesson in personal transformation, resilience, and the power of nurturing one's inner potential.

————————-

38.

QUESTION AND ANSWER(Q & A) SESSION WITH JP

This conversation is a Q&A session with Jayaprakash Nagathihalli during a Personality Transformation Workshop, where various participants ask him insightful questions related to life, success, and personal development. Here's a summary of the key points covered:

1. Life's Purpose and Success: Jayaprakash emphasizes that life is about choices. Between birth and death, what really matters is how we choose to live. He states, **"Life is time, and time is life,"** meaning that the quality of our life is shaped by how we use our time.

2. Community Impact: In response to Sadashiv's question about rural awareness and improvement, Jayaprakash highlights the importance of bringing transformation to rural areas, especially through camps and programs that can help educate and uplift people. He himself has traveled to many districts in Karnataka, especially in North Karnataka, and encourages local leaders to take the initiative.

3. The Secret to Success: When asked by Suputra about the secret to success, Jayaprakash explains that success is like a key that unlocks doors. He talks about six key elements for personality development: physical, mental, intellectual, emotional, spiritual, and financial. He suggests focusing on the element that is most needed for your life.

4. Philosophy and Personal Development: Shankar asks about the six philosophies (physical, mental, intellectual, emotional, spiritual, and financial). Jayaprakash stresses the importance of understanding and nurturing these aspects of life. He further explains the physical aspect, describing the human body as our "permanent address" in life, and mentions the importance of taking care of our health through proper understanding.

5. Future Workshops: Regarding Shankar's question about continuing workshops, Jayaprakash confirms that workshops will continue, and a new workshop called "Old Wine in a New Bottle" will start on June 7th.

This exchange demonstrates a deep focus on practical wisdom, emphasizing the importance of making choices, taking care of one's physical and mental health, and making a difference in society. Jayaprakash encourages people to explore their potential and continuously work on personal transformation.

This excerpt is a fascinating and deeply insightful conversation that touches on various aspects of life, health, personal growth, and spirituality. It reflects the wisdom and experiences of Jayaprakash Nagathihalli, who offers guidance on how to live a fulfilling life. Here's a summary of the key points covered in the conversation:

1. Physical Health and Well-being:

- Jayaprakash emphasizes the importance of taking care of the body, noting that the body will support us if we nourish and care for it properly. This includes exercising regularly and making mindful decisions about what we eat.

- He highlights the interconnectedness of mind and body, suggesting that a healthy body can significantly enhance mental and emotional well-being.

2. Intellectual Growth:

- He advocates for continuous intellectual development, using decision-making and problem-solving skills to navigate life effectively. Intellectual growth, according to Jayaprakash, helps in reinventing ourselves and moving towards higher levels of personal fulfilment.

3. Emotional and Spiritual Health:

- The importance of emotional connections, like love, trust, and empathy, is stressed. He believes that material wealth does not provide the same level of satisfaction as deep, meaningful relationships.

- Spiritual practices such as prayer, meditation, and self-reflection are vital for inner peace and connecting with a higher power. He mentions that by being good, positive, and humane, individuals can attract positive energies into their lives.

4. Financial Well-being:

- He discusses the lessons learned during the COVID pandemic, particularly the distinction between "needs" and "wants." Jayaprakash advises focusing on the essentials and avoiding greed, which ultimately leads to a simpler, more content life.

5. Book of Life:

- Jayaprakash compares life to a book with chapters, where birth and death are the cover and final pages, respectively. He emphasizes the importance of consciously crafting the chapters in between learning, growing, and prioritizing what truly matters.

6. Dealing with Judgment:

- Addressing the concept of LKK syndrome (Log Kya Kahenge - "What will people say?"), he encourages individuals to pursue their dreams without worrying about others' opinions. He shares how family members sometimes hinder their progress and advocates for mutual support within families.

7. Time Management and Discipline:

- Jayaprakash shares his personal time-management approach, outlining how he prioritizes tasks and ensures productivity while still making time for personal growth and enjoyment. He encourages setting a schedule and sticking to it to make the most of each day.

8. Travel and Inspiration:

- The discussion also touches on the places Jayaprakash finds inspiring, including beautiful travel destinations such as Karwar, Sykes Point, and Dubai's Palm Grove Island. These places provide him with tranquility, a sense of connection with nature, and inspiration for personal growth.

9. Books vs. People:

- While Jayaprakash acknowledges the value of books, he stresses that his greatest learning comes from interacting with people. He has studied thousands of individuals and believes that real wisdom lies in understanding and learning from human experiences.

In conclusion, Jayaprakash encourages us to embrace life with awareness, discipline, and positivity. His teachings invite us to lead a balanced life nourishing the body, mind, and soul and to make conscious choices that contribute to our overall well-being and personal growth.

This text is a transcript from a workshop or seminar led by Jayaprakash Nagathihalli. The conversation includes multiple questions and answers about various aspects of personal development, including gratitude, habits, hobbies, mindset, and personality transformation. Let's summarize the key points:

1. **Attitude of Gratitude**: Jayaprakash emphasizes the importance of gratitude, stating that if we forget the people who help us in life, we are not truly living. He believes that showing gratitude is crucial for personal growth and that it should be reflected in one's attitude and actions.

2. **Training for Success**: He shares his experience of training diverse groups, from high school students to scientists and top-level individuals. He highlights how continuous learning and sharing knowledge with others is a key to success. For him, the joy comes from seeing others grow and succeed.

3. **Habits and Hobbies**: Jayaprakash stresses that both habits and hobbies are essential to success. However, hobbies become valuable only when they are cultivated into habits. For example, he mentions the habit of painting and how consistent practice can lead to personal achievement.

4. **Mindset and Confidence**: Regarding maintaining mental stability, he explains that self-confidence leads to inner stability. A person who consistently displays confidence is someone who has inner strength and resilience, which is essential for success in any endeavour.

5. **Personality Transformation**: He talks about the difference between personality development and personality transformation. While development involves

gradual improvement, transformation is a more profound, positive change in one's attitude and behaviour. He encourages his participants to focus on positive transformation for lasting change.

The overall message is that continuous personal development, gratitude, cultivating good habits, and focusing on positive transformations lead to success and fulfillment in life.

Is there any particular part of the conversation you'd like more insight into?

This dialogue is a rich conversation about personal development and the mindset required for transforming one's personality. Here's a summary of the key points and insights shared by Jayaprakash Nagathihalli and others:

1. **Components of Personality Development**: Jayaprakash divides personality development into six key aspects:
   - **Physical**: Your physical health and appearance.
   - **Mental**: Your mindset and emotional stability.
   - **Intellectual**: Your knowledge and how you use it.
   - **Emotional**: Your emotional intelligence and ability to manage feelings.
   - **Spiritual**: Your connection to a higher purpose or values.
   - **Financial**: How you manage and grow your resources.

1. **Overcoming Negative Personality**: It's essential to continuously work on all these aspects. If you focus on improving these six areas, you'll see a positive change in

your personality. You need to constantly reflect, re-invent yourself, and focus on personal growth.

2. **Self-Realization and Personal Reinvention**: Personal transformation starts with understanding how you're different from others. Reinventing yourself involves continuous self-reflection and upgrading your knowledge, skills, and mindset.

3. **The Role of Emotions in Personality Development**: The importance of emotional maturity is emphasized. You need to develop the ability to control your emotions, especially in difficult situations, to maintain a positive and balanced personality.

4. **The Power of Positive Thinking**: A positive outlook allows you to deal with life's challenges effectively. For instance, Jayaprakash speaks about dealing with setbacks by focusing on solutions instead of stressing over problems.

5. **Overcoming Public Speaking and Stage Fear**: Fear of public speaking is common but can be overcome with practice, comfort, and experience. As emphasized by Murali, the way you present yourself, your body language, tone of voice, and confidence is key to effective communication.

6. **Dealing with Mistakes and Criticism**: The importance of perseverance is highlighted. While people may remember mistakes, true achievers are the ones who

keep moving forward, regardless of setbacks. The focus should be on progress, not perfection.

7. **The Importance of Patience**: Patience is a crucial virtue for success. It's not just about tolerating situations but understanding that everything has its time. Like the saying "Talidavanu Baliyanu" (Patience rewards), one's efforts bear fruit with time.

8. **The Key to Leadership**: Developing habits of self-discipline, time management, learning, and managing power and resources is essential to becoming an effective leader.

The overall message is that personality transformation is a holistic process, involving all aspects of life, and requires consistent effort and patience. The focus should be on self-improvement in all areas to achieve success in both personal and professional life.

This passage is a transcript of a conversation between Lokesha and Jayaprakash Nagatihalli, which revolves around the idea of self-worth, contributing to society, and adapting to challenges like the COVID-19 pandemic.

Here's a brief summary:

1. **Self-Worth and Confidence**: Jayaprakash emphasizes that one should consider oneself as a "VIP" (Very Important Person) in life, not in an arrogant sense but by recognizing one's value and potential. This shift in

mindset helps boost confidence, especially when interacting with other people, including VIPs.

2. **Contributions During COVID-19**: Muralidhar's question focuses on how volunteers and selfless workers (like nurses and doctors) can serve society during the COVID pandemic while ensuring their own safety. Jayaprakash emphasizes the importance of following expert advice, acting with courage, and understanding the significance of one's profession in contributing to society. He applauds front-line workers and volunteers for their dedication.

3. **Life Lessons from the Pandemic**: Jayaprakash reflects on the lessons COVID-19 has taught, such as the importance of "simple living and high thinking." He advocates for minimalism carrying less luggage in life, both literally and figuratively, in order to enjoy life more fully. This philosophy applies to both material possessions and mental burdens.

4. **Inspiration and Motivation**: He encourages the audience to keep asking questions, seeking answers, and learning from various sources whether through Google, books, or discussions. He concludes by promoting his YouTube channel, where he shares motivational content.

In essence, the talk is about self-reflection, the importance of giving back to society, and how to navigate life's challenges with simplicity and courage.

———————————

39.

JP & HIS MENTORSHIP

The program emphasizes personal growth, transformation, and practical guidance on how to lead a more effective life. Key topics in the training include self-awareness, goal clarity, positive thinking, and practical applications of personality development. These transformations are seen not only in personal lives but also in professional and social settings.

Many testimonials in the text highlight the changes in both teachers and students after attending such training. It mentions several specific benefits of the program, such as:

1. **Clarity in Goals and Profession**
2. **Awareness of Career Opportunities and Entrepreneurial Mindset**
3. **Improved Communication Skills**
4. **Positive Thinking and Self-Confidence**
5. **Self-Realization and Social Awareness**
6. **Personal and Professional Transformation**

The text also provides insights into the trainers efforts to spread knowledge and guidance through online channels like YouTube and Offline workshops.

The testimonials further underscore JP's approach to personal growth as impactful, where many individuals transformed not just their approach to work but also their mindset toward life.

In short, the training program focuses on leading a purposeful life, improving one's character, and applying practical wisdom to create personal success. There are also numerous references to JP's books and their direct impact on people's lives.

____

40.

UNSUNG HERO JP
- INTERVIEW BY RAMSUNDAR

Ram:

Millions of people walk into this world to take something and go. But there are very few people who walk into this world to give back something, and these people who give back are known as change makers. The unknown change makers.

Hello I'm Ram, humour Ram. today's changemaker you know who? It is Jayaprakash Nagathihalli. And we call him JP, a guy you know what change maker he did? He left a Government job and became a trainer! Let's go and ask him. Welcome JP to my program the unknown change maker. It's really a pleasure to have you in my show and I really was wondering, one of the best jobs you know like the government job, you know, you just left it like that, and then became a trainer!

Jayaprakash Nagathihalli:

That program changed my life" I just asked him "what happened?" "Sir, I was about to commit suicide. In fact, I switched on the TV, so it has made me quit this attempt. You saved my life." So, this has haunted me like anything. So, my words can save one's life, I can identify the purpose of my life. Instead of being in a government job, it is better to be open for the global level for the public, for the utility, for the motivation, for the transformation that has triggered in me. And I wrote a book on the same topic in Kannada Solugalige Anjadiri, it has been translated into English as FEAR NOT FAILURES.

Ram:

It's really a challenging job, you know. So, can you share something?

Jayaprakash Nagathihalli:

You have asked a very right question. As many of my friends knew about this, I was a government employee. I had a passion towards training, The passion came from an International training certificate through JCI University USA, which gave me confidence. It transformed me. I conducted TV shows as a TV host for Bengaluru Doordarshan. After watching one of my shows on "Fear not Failures" one person called me and said :

"Sir, After watching your 'Fear not Failures' show I was able to overcome suicidal tendency. Like this I have received more than 500 calls and many people visited personally and told me your book has helped me like anything." So my words, my writings, have got the power of transforming the people. So, that encouraged me a lot and that resulted in saying goodbye to the government job and I continue with this training. And this passion has made me happier than my earlier life. And in fact, being in the field of training I feel the first beneficiary is Mr. Jayaprakash, then after my transformation or my motivation, I am able to motivate or transform other people, this is the idea behind it. And you have asked me another question - are you sustaining without a job? Yes Ram 90%, I have sailed through life. 10% here and there, a lot of fluctuations. I accept those fluctuations also; and I experience the same. In fact, Covid has made all of us to be equal throughout the globe. So, I'm experiencing that also. That has made me decide what to come or to learn from the online courses. I have never gone through a Zoom session. I have not yet opened or downloaded many of the courses. But this period has made me rethink and reach to the global extent. I'm very active in social media now and people are recognizing me as a Social media Influencer. I have two YouTube channels Jayaprakash Nagathihalli in Kannada and Transformation Unlimited in English followed by 55,000 subscribers and I have more than 12,000 followers on LinkedIn, I'm also at Facebook and Instagram and X. So, anybody who wants to connect with me, please connect with me by just searching Jayaprakash Nagathihalli.

Ram:

Hey JP, what an inspiring Journey you know! Wow! It was really very inspiring! But you are mentioning online and all. Today the trend itself has become like online. But how are you coping up with the global audience and all about it? Can you share something about that?

Jayaprakash Nagathihalli:

Today, I just observed the analytics of my YouTube. I observed that I have a fan following of around 70 countries.

Ram: Wow!

Jayaprakash Nagathihalli: The US is number one and Vietnam is number two.

Ram: Vietnam!

Jayaprakash Nagathihalli:
I was surprised, Ram. So, we do not know. See, it is our duty, okay, to be online, that means we are exposed to the whole globe. That means the whole globe is at our hand.

Ram: Very true, very true.

Jayaprakash Nagathihalli:

Okay? I do...... guide the people to go online and this is the best time to go for it.

Ram: But how are you planning for this?

Jayaprakash Nagathihalli:

I'm taking different opinions from the experts in this field. I'm Consulting and I do observe, I do study others who are in my field. So, it will automatically come into the...... So, I'll take the best practices of other trainers. If I take one point from each trainer we can shape our own course. So, in the similar way only I have designed a course on personality development for 3 months after studying for 8 months.

Ram:

Wow! Okay. That's great! So what do you say a message for these young people today you know, they are all under the fear of this pandemic and all. They don't know how to cope up with this. And is there any message you would like to give to the viewers?

Jayaprakash Nagathihalli:

Through online I have seen a person who is earning six lakhs per month on YouTube.

Ram: Okay.

Jayaprakash Nagathihalli:

He is just a SSLC pass out and the person who is not having proper communication, that person is earning six lakhs! Then what are we doing? So, there is a message. They might not tell us the whole story behind it, but if you are entering step by step now, we'll come to know, if you enter the first step then it will take us to the second step. So, after the second step we can definitely go to the third step. So, without making an effort, nothing will happen. So, take that first step. It will take you to the next level, learn and then you can earn, and then you can be happy as well."

Ram:

Wow, what a message! Thank you JP for being in my show and it's really wonderful hosting you. I can proudly say, **"JP is really a change maker.**

Ram:

Thank you. That was Jayaprakash Nagathihalli. What an inspiring journey!

____

Author's Introduction

JAYAPRAKASH NAGATHIHALLI

- Transformation MENTOR
- International TRAINER
- Best Selling AUTHOR
- Social Media INFLUENCER

Email: smilingjp@gmail.com

Mobile: +91 9886081188

————————————

TRAINER

- International Trainer
- 30+ years of rich training experience
- Trained over 10 Lakhs people so far.
- Online: Silver, Gold, Diamond & Platinum Modules
- Offline: ONE DAY & THREE DAYS Workshops
- Associated with many reputed Educational Institutions, Government, Private, Corporate and NGO's .

————————————

SPECIALIZATION

Public Speaking
Communication / Life Skills
Personality Development etc.,
Customized Training Workshops

————————————

AUTHOR OF KANNADA BOOKS

1. Nudigannadi
2. Solugalige Anjadiri
3. Keelarime
4. Anukshana Anubhavisi
5. Udyoga Koushalyagalu
6. Tiruvugala Arivu
7. Ananyate Ariyiri
8. Sadhakara Chandana
9. Sahitya Chandana
10. Vyaktitva Chandana

11. Nirupane Rirupisi
12. Jeevanothsaha
13. Lifu Namdene
14. Vyaktitva Darpana
15. Vyaktitva Parivartane

—————————————

TRANSLATED TO ENGLISH

1. Fear Not Failures
2. Inferiority Complex
3. Celebrate Every Moment

Books are available with
SAPNA BOOK HOUSE
(www.sapnaonline.com)

—————————————

VIDEOS ON

1. Humour
2. Examination
3. Failures to Success
4. Overcome Inferiority Complex
5. Be Happy
6. Be an Entrepreneur
7. Positive Attitude
8. Speech is Pearl
9. Enthusiasm
10. Turning Point
11. Unwanted
12. Art of Parenting

—————————————

AUDIOS ON

1. Personality Development
2. Time Management
3. Melody of Life
4. Self Confidence
5. Short Poems
6. Happy Married Life

[Audios & Videos produced by Nagamma Foundation (R)
- Please Call +91 934 125 9267 to purchase Soft Copies]
—————————

SOCIAL MEDIA INFLUENCER

YOUTUBE CHANNELS
- Jayaprakash Nagathihalli & Transformation Unlimited - Over 55,000 SUBSCRIBERS
—————————

CONTINUOUS MOTIVATION & TRANSFORMATION THROUGH VARIOUS TOPICS.
Uploaded more than 5,000 Videos till date.
—————————

ENTREPRENEUR

Proprietor, Transformation Unlimited
—————————

PHILANTHROPIST

Founder, Nagamma Foundation ®
—————————

GRATITUDE FUNCTION
- Recognized more than 200 achievers till this year.
––––––––––

PAST EXPERIENCES – ORGANIZER

Overall organized more than 500 cultural and literary programmes for the community.
1. President, Youth Writers & Artists Guild - 10 years.
2. President, Junior Chamber International &
Zone Officer for 1 + 2 years.
3. Indo-Soviet Cultural Society
4. Karnataka State Peace & Solidarity Organization
5. Program Committee Member, Bharatiya Vidya Bhavan
––––––––––––

MEDIA TV HOST

Anchored programmes on Chandana TV, Bangalore Doordarshan and interviewed more than 1,500 personalities for Television.
News reader for 3 years.
––––––––––

RADIO

Presented more than 300 Radio programmes for Bangalore All India Radio.
Presented the Talk Series 'Solugalige Anjadiri'[FEAR NOT FAILURES] for Radio City FM.
Presented motivational series for Jnanavani FM.
––––––––––

STAGE SHOWS

Anchored more than 1,000 programmes.

ACTING

Acted in dramas, serials and movies.

KARATE

Trained by Dr.A.K. Atre, Former Principal,
Vijaya College, Black Belt Holder trained for 4 years.

WORKING TOWARDS PASSION

Gave up job in the Commercial Tax Department and became a
full-time trainer in 2008.

QUALIFICATION

Science - Arts - Commerce - Training.
1. B.Sc., from Bangalore University.
2. Masters Degree in Mass Communication & Journalism &
Diploma in Journalism
3. Diploma in Business Administration- 3 years
4. Excel Graduation from JCI University USA.

AWARDS

- Best District Youth Award
- Best Trainer of the year Award - Gurupuraskar
- Motivational Guru Award
- Super Achiever
- World Best Citizen Award
- Dr. Ambedkar Ratna Award
- Chanakya Award
- Sir M. Vishweshwaraiah Award
- Honoured by more than 1000 organizations
- Karnataka Rajyotsava Award by U CAN V CAN

——————————

VISION

- To train 2 million people.
- Be a Mentor for more achievers.
- To write more books.
- To inspire and transform through meaningful content in social media.
- Creating more Online Courses

——————————

Artist's Introduction

PRAVEEN RABAKAVI

Mr. Praveen Rabakavi is originally a theatre artist who received training at the Neenasam Theatre School and graduated from there. He has acted in more than 30 plays and worked with renowned directors such as Sri B.V. Karanth, Sri Girish Kasaravalli, Sri Girish Karnad, Sri Chandrashekar Kambar, and Sri K. Raghavendra Rao.

He is not only a talented actor but also an exceptional artist. He has worked as an illustrator for several popular magazines, including *Noothana, Mayura, Sudha, Mayadarpana, Hi Bangalore, Aakruti*, and various local publications.

Currently, he is active in both television and cinema as an actor, while also engaging in direction, art direction, and writing. Actor-thinker Praveen Rabakavi has contributed meaningful and symbolic illustrations to complement this work (chapters). This is a matter of pride for us. His illustrations have added even more brilliance to this creation, which is no exaggeration.

Disclaimer

This book is for educational purposes only. Readers acknowledge that the author does not render legal, financial, medical, or professional advice. The content within this book has been derived from various sources. Please consult a licensed professional before attempting any techniques outlined in this book.

By reading this document, the reader agrees that under no circumstances is the author responsible for any direct or indirect losses incurred as a result of the use of the information contained within this document, including but not limited to errors, omissions, or inaccuracies.

Adherence to all applicable laws and regulations, including international, federal, state, and local governing professional licensing, business practices, advertising, and all other jurisdictions, is the sole responsibility of the purchaser or reader. Neither the author nor the publisher assumes any responsibility or liability whatsoever on behalf of the purchaser or reader of these materials. Any perceived slight of any individual or organization is purely unintentional.

www.ingramcontent.com/pod-product-compliance
Lightning Source LLC
Chambersburg PA
CBHW040750120726

48005CB00012B/1124